The big story

The big story

10 studies in Luke
for individuals and groups

Introduced by Nigel Lee

Edited by Ro Willoughby

Written by
Jo Bramwell, Colin Duriez,
David Healey, David Stone,
and Ro Willoughby

Inter-Varsity Press

INTER-VARSITY PRESS
38 De Montfort Street, Leicester LE1 7GP, UK

Unless otherwise stated, Scripture quotations in this publication are from the Holy Bible, New International Version. Copyright © 1973, 1978, 1984 International Bible Society. Published in Great Britain by Hodder and Stoughton Ltd.

'Why did Jesus have to die?' by Donald Bridge is taken from John Balchin *et al.* (eds.), *The Bible User's Manual* (Inter-Varsity Press and Scripture Union, 1991), pp. 270–272.

The Word List and part of 'Dr Luke and his gospel' are adapted from material by Nigel Lee and Colin Duriez in *Don't Judge a Book by its Cover*, an edition of the New International Version of Luke's gospel (Bible Society and UCCF, 1994).

First published 1994

British Library Cataloguing in Publication Data
A catalogue record for this book is available from the British Library.

ISBN 0-85111-150-5

Photoset in Great Britain by Parker Typesetting Service, Leicester.
Printed in Great Britain by Cox & Wyman Ltd, Reading.

Inter-Varsity Press is the book-publishing division of the Universities and Colleges Christian Fellowship (formerly the Inter-Varsity Fellowship), a student movement linking Christian Unions in universities and colleges throughout the United Kingdom and the Republic of Ireland, and a member movement of the International Fellowship of Evangelical Students. For information about local and national activities write to UCCF, 38 De Montfort Street, Leicester LE1 7GP.

Contents

Introducing Luke

The third gospel is one of the very earliest lives of Jesus, and remains one of the easiest to read. It's by Luke, who had a writer's instinct about how to tell the big story. His purpose was to explain Christianity in an orderly way so that his friend Theophilus, for whom he wrote, could make his own mind up about Jesus in a few hours. It became one of the most widely read short books ever to be written, proving to be much more than just a simple biography.

Luke reads like a modern film script. We move from one quick scene to another. The link is provided by the emerging character and stories of the one who was eventually crucified as the self-proclaimed 'Son of God', and then provided the ultimate happy ending.

Luke has established a high reputation as a historian. Wherever modern scholarship has been able to check up on the accuracy of Luke's work the judgment has been impressive; he is one of the best historians in the ancient world. As he claims in his opening paragraph, Luke is setting out to write a carefully researched report on the life of Jesus so that his reader can be sure of what the eyewitnesses experienced.

Luke wanted his readers to become Christians. He did not set out a series of philosophical arguments for the existence of God or for Christian principles. Instead he put together a selection of documentary 'clips' of Jesus in action so that people could see and hear him for themselves. Luke senses that we can trust someone only when we start to know that person in ordinary life. This is what happens when we read Luke's book – we start to get to know Jesus and the secret of his pulling power.

Nigel Lee

How to use this guide

In Luke's unfolding story, people of all kinds encounter Jesus. These studies are aimed at providing a way into his story of Jesus, the people involved, Jesus' teaching, and the meaning of his life, death, and resurrection.

The Big Story is designed to bring us into contact with God's Word in the pages of Luke, so that we can be transformed by its message. We are shown its relevance to our lives today.

An important feature of *The Big Story* is that it combines the best of inductive and directive methods of Bible study. You are encouraged to encounter Scripture first-hand for yourself, but you are not cast adrift and left simply to your own resources.

The studies leave spaces for your own response, but also have plenty of information and guidance, including sections which open up themes or features of Luke's gospel. There is, in addition, a handy Word List at the end of the book, and extensive notes for group leaders.

Luke is the longest book of the New Testament, so it is not possible to cover all of it in ten sessions. Instead, a careful selection of passages has been made for the studies, representing the concerns of Luke's gospel, particularly his interest in the people who feature in the events of Jesus' life.

The ten studies can be used in a term or semester at university or college, or for a season of church mid-week house groups or similar meetings.

Suggestions for individual study

1. When you begin each session, ask God for help in understanding the passage or passages, and in applying his Word to your life.

2. It is helpful to use a good modern translation, such as the New International Version. This guide is based on the NIV.

3. Read the passage or passages more than once to become familiar with what Luke is saying. If you really know what the passages are saying you are much more likely to have a reasonably good understanding of them.

4. Don't be embarrassed to write down your answers in the spaces provided. Expressing your understanding deepens and tests it. This shows a willingness to come to grips with God's Word, around which the questions are based.

5. After you have made your notes, use the corresponding notes at the end of the book for further insights.

6. Have good resource books handy, such as a Bible dictionary. Unfamiliar words, names, places or ideas can be looked up. Also, use the Word List and the thematic sections in this book.

7. At the end of each session is a section entitled 'Going further'. This gives you some work to do between sessions, to reinforce what you have learnt and to take your understanding on further. It includes a 'memory verse' for you to learn by heart, which encapsulates the study's main point.

Suggestions for group study

1. Make a point of coming to the session prepared. It is important to follow the suggestions for individual study given above. The group session will be far richer as a result of careful individual preparation.

2. Some people by temperament find it easy to participate in group discussion, but others find it difficult. Decide in advance that you are going to participate, drawing on the fruits of your individual study. Your group leader will be inviting the group members to discuss what they have discovered in the passage(s) from Luke for the session. The leader will be using questions from this guide.

3. Make an effort to keep to the passage(s) for the session. Your answers should derive from the verses which are the focus of the session.

4. Tune into the other members of your group. Listen attentively to what they say as they tell you of their discoveries in the passage(s). When you say something, try hard to link it into the comments of other members. This will help the group not to drift away from the focus of the session.

5. Avoid dominating the discussion, but do participate. Encourage others to participate by affirming their contributions.

6. Be expectant that God will teach you through the passage(s) being studied. After all, they are part of his Word! Expect too that you will learn from the others in the group. Pray that your encounter with his Word will help you meet God, and that there will be changes in your life as a result.

Group leaders

At the end of this guide there are specific suggestions which will help leaders of each session.

People at the beginning of the story

Luke: 1:26–38; 2:1–20

Luke is the gospel writer who tells of the angel's visit to Mary. Most of the subsequent details of Jesus' birth are also unique to him. Matthew is the only other New Testament writer who gives any account of Jesus' birth.

The angel Gabriel's announcement must have come as a complete shock to Mary. There is a stark contrast between her ordinariness and the entrance of the supernatural into her life. She was a young Jewish girl, living in a small out-of-the-way town in Northern Palestine. She was engaged to a man who was of the same Jewish tribe, Judah, the tribe of David. It was not a loose agreement as engagements tend to be today in the West; her betrothal was legally binding. But, until the actual marriage, the relationship would not have been consummated. The angel's message to her was that, although still a virgin, she would carry and give birth to a child who would be fully human. He would be her future husband's son in a legal sense only. This was truly divine.

Luke has a concern for historical landmarks, which gives his writings an authenticity. Thus he places the account in a definite point in history. A census was being demanded by the occupying Roman forces. That meant that the couple were required to travel over 70 miles to Bethlehem, their place of origin. This is how the prophecy was fulfilled which declared that the Messiah would be born in the 'city of David'.

The birth was ordinary enough. Contrary to popular folklore, the fact that Jesus was born in a place surrounded by animals is not evidence that he was born in abject poverty. Families and animals frequently shared the same accommodation. There was nothing out of the ordinary here. What *was* extraordinary was the dazzling appearance of angels to shepherds on the hills above Bethlehem.

So from his earliest days, Jesus is surrounded by a variety of people, of all ages, of both sexes, of differing ethnic backgrounds, status, wealth, health and position before God. All of them interact with Jesus, with differing results. And all of them, if honest, have to admit that this man who appeared to be fairly ordinary is in fact quite the opposite.

Opening up

1. Christmas-card pictures, television and church services leave us with a variety of impressions of Jesus' birth. What images are you left with? (Think of location, lighting, emotional effects, personnel, *etc*.)

How much are these images a product of tradition or the Bible's account? Remember that Matthew also gives a record of the birth. Most traditional pictures conflate the two accounts.

Looking at a few of the people who were around at Jesus' birth (which we shall be doing in this study) may alter some of your perceptions of the Christmas story.

Exploring the story

Read Luke 1:26–38

2. Mary was a young girl (maybe no more than thirteen.)

What else do we know about her? Why should we not be surprised that she was so troubled (verse 29)?

3. Make a list of each of the instructions that the angel gave to Mary.

4. Often, when we first hear dramatic news, we find it hard to absorb all the details. Which of these instructions do you think Mary would find particularly hard to accept or understand?

Verses 28–33: Mary is 'highly favoured'. God had chosen her to bear a son, Jesus (equivalent to 'Joshua' in Hebrew, meaning 'saviour'; see 'Salvation', p. 60). The expressions used of Jesus, such as 'Son of the Most High', indicated he was the Messiah, though the word is not used (see 'Jesus in the Old Testament', p. 20).

5. Our reactions in a crisis often reveal what we are really like. What does Mary's reaction show of the true character of the woman who was to be Jesus' mother?

6. This was only the start of what God was going to do in her life. What is God doing in your life at the moment? Has he put you in a situation which is demanding, life-changing, un-welcome or unexpected? How have you responded?

7. 'I am the Lord's servant,' Mary answered. 'May it be to me as you have said' (Luke 1:38). How far are Mary's words of submission to God's will applicable to you?

Read Luke 2:1–20
8. You could be excused for thinking that angels were in the habit of scaring people witless! Instructions to the shepherds

(verses 10–12) were less complicated than those to Mary. What were they?

Shepherds did not usually own their own sheep but were hired men. It was in their interests to protect the sheep from loss or scavengers. But the romantic pastoral image of Jewish shepherds we may have is quite misplaced. They were on the fringe of society, notorious for their unlawful activities such as thieving. As is so often the case with Luke, he highlights the marginalized in society, such as the poor, Samaritans, and women.

---

9. What was *the shepherds'* reaction? Put in your own words how they would have come to understand that this was God in action.

10. The responses of Mary and the shepherds to their encounter with the baby Jesus were different (verses 19, 20), but equally understandable. When you have seen God in action has your response been more like Mary's or the shepherds'? How far can we combine the two?

Thinking back

11. Returning to your impressions at the start of this study, reflect on what you have just read. What images of the Christmas story now strike you?

Going further

12. A song at Christmas: read Luke 1:1–25; 39–56. Then look up 1 Samuel 2:1–10; could Hannah's song have influenced Mary?

13. In verses 46–49 what do you see of Mary's response and relationship with God in the light of her circumstances?

14. Mary would have known her Old Testament stories of how God had dealt with his people in the past. She would be looking forward to the glorious age to come. What specific examples of

God's dealings with his people might she be remembering? (For instance, verse 51 could refer to the exodus, when God delivered the people of Israel from slavery in Egypt.)

Memory verse
Luke 1:38: ' "I am the Lord's servant," Mary answered. "May it be to me as you have said." '

Jesus in the Old Testament

The Old Testament has to deal with one very difficult issue: how to come to terms with the fact that God's people seemed to be past their best.

The Old Testament writers faced this in two ways. First, they explained the decline in terms of the people's sin. The difficulties faced by the Jews resulted from God's judgment on their failure to keep his law. Secondly, they expressed the hope that the decline was only temporary and that, sooner or later, God would step in and restore them to the glory of earlier and happier times.

In particular, they looked back to Israel's golden age under King David. This is what lies behind later Jewish expectations of the Messiah (a Hebrew word whose Greek equivalent is Christ). Right through the Old Testament are passages which, as well as having direct application at the time when they were written, can also be applied to this future hope of a Messiah which developed towards the end of the Old Testament period. By the time of Jesus, the occupation of Palestine by the Romans had given even greater impetus to messianic aspirations. It seemed to many that Jesus, with his strong public following and ability to perform mighty miracles, fitted the bill nicely.

What does Luke make of all this? The answer is that he gives several indications of his conviction that Jesus is indeed the Messiah, but that his messiahship is rather different from what his fellow Jews were expecting.

To begin with, the prophecies around Jesus' birth point to his special identity. Mary's song focuses on the way that Jesus will be the fulfilment of God's promise of mercy to the descendants of Abraham (Luke 1:54–55). Zechariah makes the same point (Luke 1:72–73) as he looks forward to the promised salvation of God's people through a descendant of David (Luke 1:68–69).

One strand of messianic expectation was that the Messiah would be preceded by the arrival of the prophet Elijah. This explains why John the Baptist is described as operating 'in the spirit and power of Elijah' (1:17; see also 9:8). His task is 'to make ready a people prepared for the Lord', an aspect which Zechariah repeats in Luke 1:76. Luke stresses this again by quoting the relevant prophecy from Isaiah 40 when commenting on John the Baptist's ministry (Luke 3:4–6; see also 7:27).

Luke goes on to underline the fact that Jesus is a direct descendant of King David and so qualified to sit on his throne. The angel Gabriel announces to Mary that 'The Lord God will give him the throne of his father David, and he will reign over the house of Jacob for ever; his kingdom will never end' (Luke 1:32–33; see also 1:27, 69; 2:4, 11; 3:31; 18:38–39; 20:41–44). Towards the end of his public ministry, Jesus clearly illustrates this claim as he rides into Jerusalem on a donkey. This action recalls the messianic prophecy of Zechariah 9:9: 'Rejoice greatly, O Daughter of Zion! Shout, Daughter of Jerusalem! See, your king comes to you, righteous and having salvation, gentle and riding on a donkey, on a colt, the foal of a donkey.'

Furthermore, Jesus is specifically identified as the Messiah or Christ on several occasions (see 2:11, 26; 4:41; 9:20; 22:67; 23:2, 35, 39; 24:26, 46). As he begins his public ministry, he quotes directly from the messianic prophecy in Isaiah 61 and applies it to himself (Luke 4:16–21). Later, when John the Baptist expresses uncertainty about whether or not Jesus is really 'the one who was to come', Jesus replies by quoting another messianic prophecy, this time from Isaiah 35 (Luke 7:18–23).

But Jesus is quick to scotch popular misconceptions about what this means. His mission runs far deeper than simply rescuing Israel from the grip of Rome: his goal is to release the whole world from the grip of Satan! And so, as soon as the penny has dropped for Peter and his fellow disciples, Jesus goes on to enjoin secrecy (to avoid misunderstanding) and to explain that 'the Son of Man must suffer many things and be rejected by the elders, chief priests and teachers of the law, and he must be killed and on the third day be raised to life' (Luke 9:22). Not quite what they were hoping for from a great deliverer!

As Luke points out right at the end of his gospel, it was not until after Jesus' resurrection that they fully understood. Talking with the two disciples on the road to Emmaus, Jesus chides them: '"How foolish you are, and how slow of heart to believe all that the prophets have spoken! Did not the Christ have to suffer these things and then enter his glory?" And beginning with Moses and all the Prophets, he explained to them what was said in all the Scriptures concerning himself' (Luke 24:25–27).

Later, all eleven have the benefit of the same Bible study: 'He said to them, "This is what I told you while I was still with you: Everything must be fulfilled that is written about me in the Law of Moses, the Prophets and the Psalms." Then he opened their minds so they could understand the Scriptures. He told them, "This is what is written: The Christ will suffer and rise from the dead on the third day, and repentance and forgiveness of sins will be preached in his name to all nations, beginning at Jerusalem"' (Luke 24:44–47).

Once they have caught on, there's no stopping them. As Luke reports in the Acts of the Apostles, they come back again and again to the way in which Jesus, through his fulfilment of Old Testament prophecy, can clearly be identified as the Messiah (*e.g.* Acts 2:25–28, 34; 3:18–26; 4:11, 25–27; 8:32–35; 10:43; 13:16–41; 17:2–3; 18:28; 26:22–27; 28:23).

Jesus and John the Baptist

Luke 1:57–80; 3:15–22; 7:18–35

All through the Old Testament, prophets such as Isaiah had been foretelling the arrival of the Messiah, the 'anointed one' from God. There were many opinions about what he would be like. Some expected a nationalist leader for the Jewish nation; others expected a prophet-type figure like Moses or Elijah; still others looked for one who would come as the prince of peace.

The last of these prophets was John the Baptist. Jesus gave him this accolade: 'The Law and the Prophets were proclaimed until John. Since that time, the good news of the kingdom of God is being preached' (Luke 16:16). (See 'The Kingdom of God', p. 29.)

John's task was to make the final preparations for Jesus, the Messiah, fulfilling the prophecy recorded in Malachi 3:1. He preached a radical message, condemning the present system, looking to the future and calling for repentance. Baptism, with its association with cleansing, judgment and new beginnings, was the symbol of turning from the past and claiming forgiveness of sins (see Luke 3:3). It was this role as the Baptizer which gave him his distinctive title.

The lives of John the Baptist and Jesus had been connected from before their births, because they were cousins. In this study we shall explore how closely interwoven were the lives of these two cousins and discover just how much their respective ministries complemented each other.

Opening up

1. What hopes might you have for a child born in the 1990s? Long life? Success? What else?

John's conception and the announcement of his coming birth were quite out of the ordinary and touched with the miraculous. His father, Zechariah, did not believe the angel Gabriel who informed him of the expected birth. His lack of faith led to an inability to speak until after the birth (1:20). His wife Elizabeth was more accepting (1:25), and went on to support her cousin, Mary, who was pregnant under even more extraordinary circumstances (1:42–45).

Exploring the story

Read Luke 1:57–80

2. What do we know about John's parents? What expectations did Zechariah have for his son?

3. Compare his expectations with those expectations given to Mary by Simeon, the old man of God in the temple (2:34–35).

4. Recalling the last study, make a list of the similarities and the differences in what is said about Jesus and John at their births.

> The road ahead for both sets of parents and their sons was one of pain and heartache. Yet it was the road of obedience to God. Of course, no parent today confronts issues such as these. But parenting is demanding and costly.

5. Think of Christian parents you know and pray for them and their expectations for their children, especially as they are part of God's future activity in the world. If you are not yet a parent, pray for yourself – for the role of parenting may yet be yours!

Both boys have grown up when we read of their next meeting. John is living in the wilderness, preaching the message of repentance for the forgiveness of sins. People flocked to hear him and were baptized in the River Jordan. But the hostility of his enemies was increasing – from the religious authorities to King Herod.

6. From his own preaching, how important did John regard his own ministry?

7. If you were a journalist, how would you describe the scene of Jesus' baptism?

8. What would John have understood about Jesus from the baptism?

Once Jesus had arrived, there was no place or need for John's preaching. His task was complete and he was forcibly removed. John bears a resemblance to Moses, who led the people of Israel to the edge of the promised land but never entered it. It was Joshua's task to lead the people there.

In prison John had plenty of time to think about his own ministry and that of his cousin.

9. What lay behind John's question in verse 20?

10. What things did Jesus do to help John understand?

11. If you had the opportunity, what questions would you like to ask Jesus about his life and teaching? Or what do you find hard to believe about him? Make a list of these things.

12. How far is it appropriate to ask such questions? How might you expect Jesus to respond to your questions?

Thinking back

13. Pray for those you know (including yourself) who are asking God questions.

Going further

To find out the end of John's story read Matthew 14:1–12 and Mark 6:14–29.

To continue the story of Jesus' early years, read Luke 2:21–52. Think of Simeon's song (verses 29–32) in the light of 'Jesus in the Old Testament' (p. 20) and 'Salvation' (p. 60).

Memory verse

Luke 3:22: 'The Holy Spirit descended on him in bodily form like a dove. And a voice came from heaven: "You are my Son, whom I love; with you I am well pleased."'

The kingdom of God

In Luke, and the similar gospels of Matthew and Mark, the kingdom of God is the central thrust of Jesus' teaching. It refers to God's rule or reign, the sphere of his sovereign control.

John the Baptist heralds the coming of God's kingdom. He announces that divine judgment is a reality which is immediately at hand. The axe is already laid to the roots of the trees (Luke 3:7–9). John speaks of being the forerunner to one who will bring God's judgment (Luke 3:16–17).

John's message highlights the need for immediate repentance. People must be baptized for the forgiveness of their sins, which Jesus alone could bring about through his death on the cross (see 24:46–47). In this way they would escape God's anger and be part of the salvation of the kingdom. When the kingdom comes they will be able to share in the baptism of the Holy Spirit who will be poured out.

Jesus brought in the kingdom of God. His proclamation underlines John's, but presents the full picture John hinted at. Jesus endorses the message of judgment and the need for repentance. But he goes beyond this in stressing the liberating salvation that God's kingdom brings. Jesus also is able to declare that the kingdom is no longer merely at hand, but has actually come. The evidence is in his own person and doings.

The here-and-now reality of the kingdom was demonstrated in many ways. It was shown vividly, for example, in the casting out of demons (see Luke 11:20), and underlies all Jesus' miracles. Miracles were signs of God's power and active rule over the created world. They demonstrated that the sway of Satan was being radically challenged. Such demonstrations of God's kingdom were also signs that Jesus was God's Son and God's chosen King of human beings.

As well as the dramatic impact of exorcism and Jesus' miracles, there was his proclaiming of the good news of salvation (Luke 7:22). Forgiveness for sin also was available through his ministry. Thus, when a paralysed man was lowered through the roof of a house so that Jesus could heal him, Jesus publicly stated, 'Friend, your sins are forgiven' (Luke 5:17–26).

Above all else Jesus came to seek and save the lost (Luke 19:10).

The kingdom of God is both 'now' and 'not yet'. One day Christ will return, revealed in his full glory, rather than as the King in ordinary clothes that he was during his life here. The angel was right when he told Mary about the son she would bear; 'his kingdom will never end' (Luke 1:33).

Satanic attack and evil spirits

Luke 4:1–13, 31–44

Scarcely a week goes by without the media headlines searing our minds with another horrific example of evil bubbling up to the surface in our society. It used to be fashionable to dismiss the reality of personal evil as a quaint relic of a bygone age. But nowadays people aren't so sure. What else could account for these appalling events?

Modern society seems to be returning warily to a perspective we find Luke tackling with no trace of embarrassment. For him, 'salvation from our enemies and from the hand of all that hate us' (1:71) refers just as much to the spiritual dimension as it does to anything else. And in chapter 4 of his gospel he shows how the light of Christ begins to 'shine on those living in darkness and in the shadow of death' (1:79).

Later on in the gospel, Luke will tell us what Jesus had to say about his confrontation with the devil. 'When a strong man, fully armed, guards his own house, his possessions are safe. But when someone stronger attacks and overpowers him, he takes away the armour in which the man trusted and divides up the spoils' (11:21–22). This is what has happened. Although we often see the temptations of Jesus as Satan's attacks on him, it's clear that the boot was also on the other foot as Jesus sees 'Satan fall like lightning from heaven' (10:18). This opening encounter in chapter 4 marks the beginning of the end for Satan. His reign is effectively over. Darkness is up for defeat. The light has come. From now on he will face defeat after defeat as Jesus fulfils Isaiah's prophecy and sets about his work as the great Liberator, culminating in his triumphant yet harrowing death.

Opening up

1. What sort of things do you think of as evil? Make a list of them. How would you score them out of 10? Can you go on to say why they are evil?

Exploring the story

Read Luke 4:1–13

2. What do you notice about the role of the Holy Spirit in this incident? How does this relate to your own experience recently?

3. Would it ever have been all right for Jesus to tell a stone to become bread? Why? What was wrong with turning '*this* stone' (verse 4) into bread?

4. How does Jesus respond to each of the devil's suggestions? What can his example teach us?

5. People sometimes suggest that, because he was the Son of God, it was easier for Jesus to resist temptation than it is for us. What do you think? Why?

6. Turning to the list you made in question 1, do any of the items relate to the temptation faced by Jesus? Why do you think this is?

Read Luke 4:31–44

> In Jewish tradition, the exorcism of evil spirits was seen as a mark of the rule of the Messiah. See Luke 11:14–26, especially verse 20. (See 'The Kingdom of God', p. 29.)

7. What effect does the evil spirit have on the man possessed by the demon in verse 32? How does this contrast with what you know of the activity of the Holy Spirit?

8. These days, we might be tempted to say that this man's affliction was simply a mental illness. What is there in Luke's description of the event which should make us hesitate before drawing this conclusion?

9. Verse 34 expresses the evil spirit's own understanding of its fate, a truth confirmed by 1 John 3:8: 'The reason the Son of God appeared was to destroy the devil's work.' Can you think of any aspects of the devil's work that need to be destroyed in our lives today?

10. Since a major part of Jesus' ministry is to let people know who he is, why does he refuse to let the demons speak out the truth (verse 41)?

Thinking back

11. Jesus prayed, 'Deliver us from the evil one' (Matthew 6:13). Pray, using this theme of being kept from evil, in the light of the study you've just done.

Going further

12. Consider other passages in Luke where there is direct confrontation with evil powers or satanic activity (Luke 11:14–28; 22:1–6). Do you see evidence that our society is more willing to accept the reality of spiritual powers and a spiritual dimension to life than previously? What do you think are the opportunities and dangers of such acceptance?

Memory verses
Luke 4:18–19:

> 'The Spirit of the Lord is on me,
>   because he has anointed me
>   to preach good news to the poor.
> He has sent me to proclaim freedom for the prisoners
>   and recovery of sight for the blind,
> to release the oppressed,
>   to proclaim the year of the Lord's favour.'

The Holy Spirit in Luke

Of all the gospels, Luke's places particular emphasis on the role of the Holy Spirit in the ministry of Jesus and his followers. As Luke sets out so clearly in the Acts of the Apostles, the Holy Spirit is the prime mover in the life of the early church. But we're not to think of him suddenly coming into the picture on the day of Pentecost: he was involved from the very start, bearing witness to the truth of who Jesus is and what he came to do (compare John 15:26; 16:14–15).

Luke brings this out in his gospel by describing a cluster of incidents around the birth of Jesus. These demonstrate the different ways in which the Holy Spirit acts as a witness to Jesus, both directly and indirectly as he works through others.

He begins with John the Baptist, the great forerunner of Jesus who pointed to the truth about him. His ability as a witness stemmed from the fact that he was filled by the Holy Spirit 'even from birth' (Luke 1:15). But it wasn't just him. The Holy Spirit was active in the lives of his parents too. His mother Elizabeth was 'filled with the Holy Spirit' (Luke 1:41) when she met Mary, leading her to exclaim 'in a loud voice' (Luke 1:42) and pronounce a twofold blessing on her visitor. And after John's birth, the Holy Spirit led his father, Zechariah, to utter the words of the hymn we now know as the Benedictus in Luke 1:68–79.

Notice how Luke establishes the link between being filled with the Holy Spirit and acting as God's mouthpiece, *i.e.* having the ability to prophesy (Luke 1:67). This is picked up several times in Acts (*e.g.* Acts 2:4, 11b [compare 2:16–18]; 19:6). Jesus himself encouraged his disciples with the assurance that the Holy Spirit would help them to speak out for him when under pressure: 'When you are brought before synagogues, rulers and authorities, do not worry about how you will defend yourselves or what you will say, for the Holy Spirit will teach you at that time what you should say' (Luke 12:11–12). This is certainly borne out by what happens in Acts (*e.g.* Acts 4:8).

Earlier, the angel Gabriel assured Mary that the supernatural conception of Jesus would take place through the action of the Holy Spirit, and makes a clear connection between the Spirit and 'the power of the Most High' (Luke 1:35). This accent on the divine power of the Spirit recurs several times both in Luke (4:14; 5:17; 6:19; 24:49) and Acts (1:8; 10:38).

We next meet the Holy Spirit in the life of Simeon (Luke 2:25–35). In his case, the Holy Spirit not only inspires what he has to say but is also active in revealing truth to him (2:26) and guiding him to be in the right place at the right time (2:27). Both these features of the work of the Holy Spirit recur several times in Luke's writing, especially in Acts (1:2; 7:55; 8:29; 10:19; 11:12, 28; 13:2–4; 16:6–7; 20:22–23; 21:4, 11).

Luke stresses that even the ministry of Jesus himself was dependent on his being empowered by the Spirit. At Jesus' baptism, Luke records the way in which 'the Holy Spirit descended on him in bodily form like a dove. And a voice came from heaven: "You are my Son, whom I love; with you I am well pleased"' (Luke 3:22). Subsequently, Jesus is described as being 'full of the Holy Spirit' (Luke 4:1), 'led by the Spirit' (Luke 4:1), returning to Galilee 'in the power of the Spirit' (Luke 4:14) and 'full of joy through the Holy Spirit' (Luke 10:21). At the beginning of his public ministry, he visits the synagogue in Nazareth to declare his manifesto. There he reads out and applies to himself a passage from Isaiah 61 about the good things that will happen because 'The Spirit of the Lord is upon me' (Luke 4:18).

More than that, an important aspect of the ministry of Jesus was to train and enable his followers to continue the good work he had begun. After his resurrection, Jesus commissioned them for the work of bearing witness to him: 'He told them, "This is what is written: The Christ will suffer and rise from the dead on the third day, and repentance and forgiveness of sins will be preached in his name to all nations, beginning at Jerusalem. You are witnesses of these things. I am going to send you what my Father has promised; but stay in the city until you have been clothed with power from on high"' (Luke 24:46–49).

Not that this should have come as any surprise to them. Right at the beginning, John the Baptist drew attention to this significant difference between what he was doing and what Jesus would do: 'I baptise you with water. But one more powerful than I will come, the thongs of whose sandals I am not worthy to untie. He will baptise you with the Holy Spirit and with fire' (Luke 3:16; see also Acts 1:5).

To end, a word of warning, as Luke spells out the fact that the sin of blasphemy against the Holy Spirit will not be forgiven (Luke 12:10) – not because God so chooses but because he *cannot* save those who wilfully reject the light and call it darkness. To call into question the goodness of this most wonderful of God's gifts (Luke 11:13) is a perilous thing to do.

The disciples

Luke 4:38–39; 5:1–39; 6:1–16

It must have been quite something to have been one of the disciples of Jesus during his time on earth. One of Luke's purposes in writing his gospel was to help his readers to share in what it was like. This may well be one of the factors which lies behind his dedication of the work to Theophilus – 'so that you may know the certainty of the things you have been taught' (Luke 1:4).

In this study we'll look particularly at how the events of these passages must have struck the early disciples. But this isn't just an exercise in history: Luke's gospel is God's Word for us now as much as it was for people like Theophilus then. So we'll also think about how what happened then affects us now as the latest generation of disciples.

Opening up

1. Begin by sharing together your impressions of what it means to be a disciple of Jesus. See if you can compile some sort of job description! Would you apply?

Exploring the story

Read Luke 4:38–39 and 5:1–11

Notice that what the other gospel writers call the 'Sea of Galilee', the widely travelled Luke refers to simply as the 'Lake of Gennesaret' (verse 1)! As verse 3 points out, the usual practice was for a teacher to sit and his audience to stand.

2. Jesus' command in verse 4 was rather strange, since successful fishing in deep water would usually be possible only at night. During the day they fished in shallow water. Imagine for a moment that you are Simon Peter, the experienced fisherman. What would have been going on in your mind?

3. Can you think of examples where you have felt God telling you to do something that didn't make much sense to you? How did you know it was him? And how did you respond?

> The word translated 'leprosy' here covers a number of different
> skin problems, not simply the disease we know as leprosy today.
> In accordance with Jewish law (see Leviticus 13 and 14), lepers
> were isolated from society and required to warn people of their
> approach.

4. Even though there are clearly many needs crying out to be
met, 'Jesus often withdrew to lonely places and prayed' (verse
16). Why do you think this was? What otherwise good things
tend to distract you from prayer?

Read Luke 5:17–26

5. How do you react to the suggestion that people become ill
because they sin? Does this incident support that assertion?

6. What does this incident tell us about who Jesus is? What
evidence does Luke give? Who do *you* think Jesus is? What
evidence would you give?

Read Luke 5:27–32

7. Many people have the idea that only good people can become Christians. What does this passage say about how to try and avoid giving this impression? How might you put this into practice?

8. What are the common features about following Jesus which Luke mentions in verses 11 and 27–28? How do they apply to you?

Read Luke 5:33–39

9. Looking back over this passage and the study as a whole, what was it about Jesus that so upset the Pharisees? Do these things upset others about you? Why?

10. What truth is Jesus illustrating with the pictures of patched garments and wineskins? How do they apply to you?

Read Luke 6:1–11

11. In the eyes of the Pharisees, why was it wrong for Jesus to heal on the Sabbath? Why were they 'furious' with him (verse 11)?

Read Luke 6:12–16

12. How did Jesus go about deciding which of his disciples to include in the special Twelve? What does this say to you about the way you go about making major decisions?

Thinking back

13. Thinking back to the job description you wrote in question 1, and in the light of your study session, now pray realistically for help in being Jesus' disciple in the hustle and bustle of your everyday world.

Going further

14. The circumstances today are very different from the events we've looked at in this session. But we are nevertheless to consider ourselves Jesus' disciples. Read Luke 14:25–35, which sets out the cost of being a disciple of Jesus. He is to be above all our other obligations – the Lord of every part of our lives. Meditate on his rule over different aspects of your life. For instance:

- your work
- your family (nuclear and extended)
- your studies
- your leisure time and activities
- your possessions (or lack of them!)
- your church life and CU involvement
- your thinking
- your creativity
- your emotional life and needs
- your single or married state
- your identity (in a society which generates confusion)

Memory verse
Luke 5:32: 'I have not come to call the righteous, but sinners to repentance.'

Miracles

Start reading a gospel and it isn't long before you come across a miracle – an event that cannot easily be explained by the natural laws which usually seem to govern what happens.

In Luke, the first of these occurrences is in chapter 1, where Zechariah is affected by a supernatural inability to speak as a result of his failure to believe what the angel told him (Luke 1:20). More commonly, though, we associate the gospels with the miracles performed by Jesus. Most are miracles of healing, where Jesus makes a sick person well or casts out an evil spirit. There are also three occasions in the gospels where Jesus raises someone from the dead, and a number of instances where he exercises power over the forces of nature (such as the calming of the storm in Luke 8:22–25).

Why did Jesus do these things? The answer is that his actions stemmed from and so pointed to who he was: the Son of God.

In the first place, his miracles are an expression of the *love* of God as Jesus expresses his concern for those in need. For example, Matthew 14:14 tells us that 'When Jesus landed and saw a large crowd, he had compassion on them and healed their sick.'

Secondly, the miracles are an expression of the *power* of God. The coming of Jesus heralded the arrival of God's kingdom, the ushering in of the rule of God in a new way. Since sickness and death are hallmarks of the rule of Satan, they were bound to come in for a hammering in the ministry of Jesus. An especially clear example of this is where Jesus healed a woman 'whom Satan has kept bound for eighteen long years' (Luke 13:16). The miracles signify the loosening of Satan's stranglehold on the world.

Miracles, then, are signposts which point to the identity of the one who does them and back up what he has to say. As Jesus reminds John the Baptist in Luke 7:18–23, the miracles he has been performing are simply what the Old Testament prophecies about the Messiah (in this case Isaiah 35:5–6 and 61:1–3) said he would do.

The people in the synagogue at Capernaum were impressed when they heard what Jesus had to say: 'They were amazed at his teaching, because his message had authority' (Luke 4:32). But they were even more impressed when he went on to cast out an evil spirit. For what he *did* added significantly to the authority of what he *said*: 'All the people were amazed and said to each other, "*What is this teaching?* With authority and power he gives orders to evil spirits and they come out!"' (Luke 4:36).

Another example where a healing miracle backs up the claims of Jesus is Mark 2:1–12, where Jesus was questioned about his authority to forgive the sins of a man who was brought to him. His answer was to prove it by healing the man's paralysis.

Notice that the miracles do not compel people to believe – either now or then. Plenty of Pharisees remained unconvinced! Those who say that they would believe if only they could see a miracle are mistaken. They are not absolute proofs of who Jesus is. Those who would prefer another explanation can usually find one (see Luke 11:15, for example). But they do serve as helpful pointers for those who are prepared for the consequences of believing that Jesus is who he himself and the miracles say he is.

Today, of course, people find the miracle stories hard to believe. By and large, such things just don't happen. But this is hardly relevant. The claim is not that such things happen *now* (they may do, but that's another question!), but that they happened *then*. They may be outside our normal experience, but to argue that they cannot therefore have happened is foolish. As we have seen, the miracles are entirely consistent with the claims Jesus made about his identity as God's Son. Given who he was, it would have been remarkable if he had *not* performed miracles!

Having said that, though, Luke makes it very clear that Jesus did not keep all the miracle-working to himself. The twelve apostles are given 'power and authority to drive out all demons and to cure diseases' (9:1) as Jesus sends them on a preaching tour. The same is true of the seventy-two (10:9) a chapter later.

So what about us? Christians differ sharply on whether or not we should expect the same sort of activity today. Some argue that miracles were needed at the beginning of the church's life to get things going, but that the need for them has subsequently diminished. It's true that, even within New Testament times, there seems to be less of a focus on the miraculous as time passes. Yet, although the need for miracles as evidence of the truth of Christianity may have lessened, their role as vehicles of the love and compassion of God is still important today. Maybe we should at least be asking God to work miraculously more than perhaps we do.

Faith and the non-Jew

Luke 7:1–10

As a Gentile himself, Luke is especially concerned to show that Jesus is the Saviour of the whole world, not just of the people of Israel. His gospel contains several instances which show beyond doubt that the salvation Jesus offers is available for everyone, even (or perhaps especially) for those who would have been regarded as insignificant by his fellow Jews.

It's hard for us to appreciate how negative Jews felt about Gentiles in Jesus' day. Think of apartheid in South Africa and you get some idea of what it was like. As far as possible, Gentiles were to be avoided. They were despised as idolaters and treated with great disdain. Any necessary or accidental contact would make a Jew 'unclean' and require elaborate cleansing rituals to rid them of the contamination.

How typical of God, then, to arrange that of all the people Jesus met, it was a Gentile who turned out to have the greatest faith. It's this that provides the main focus of the passage.

Opening up

1. As you look around at yourself, your family and your friends, what evidence of prejudice do you recognize? You might think of attitudes to the unemployed, the disabled, and young people begging in our city streets; the Troubles in Northern Ireland; and even the differences between northerners and southerners! What do you think such prejudices are due to?

How might such attitudes be overcome?

Exploring the story
Read Luke 7:1–10

A centurion was a Roman soldier who would have been responsible for about 100 men. This one was evidently wealthy, judging from his ability to contribute substantially to the building of the local synagogue (verse 5). Although the present-day ruin in Capernaum dates from the third century, it may well be on the same site and follow the same design as the one referred to here. Historians tell us that since Galilee was not itself part of a Roman province until AD 44, the centurion would have commanded native troops and would have served King Herod Antipas in providing a local police force. The Jews were so hostile to the ruling Herod dynasty that they were forced to keep pagan soldiers in their service.

---

2. This centurion's position among the Jews was ambivalent. On the one hand he was an officer of the hated Roman army of occupation, and his religious background was pagan. On the other, verse 4 tells us that he was so drawn to the Jewish people that he built a synagogue for them, and they esteemed him for that. What else does this passage tell us about the kind of man he was? (It might be helpful to list the information Luke gives us about his character.) Do you think you would have enjoyed meeting him? Why?

3. Despite general Jewish hostility to Gentiles, this particular one was well regarded locally. Why? On the basis of this, what advice would you give to someone who felt that he or she was the victim of prejudice?

4. Luke reports the centurion declaring himself unworthy to come to Jesus personally. Is he right? Of course, he could just be expressing oriental politeness – but what evidence is there that he really believes it?

5. Many people claim that they would believe if only they were to 'see something'. But notice that the centurion has never met or seen Jesus (verses 3, 7). On what basis, then, does he make his request? What does this have to say to us?

6. Who does the centurion think Jesus is? Why? How have you reached your own conclusion about who Jesus is?

7. In verses 7–8, the centurion is saying that he gives orders and they are carried out; similarly, if Jesus would give the order for the servant to be healed, that order would be carried out. Why do you think Jesus was 'amazed' (verse 9) at this faith?

8. If the centurion was an outsider among God's chosen people, the servant was regarded as little more than a broken-down piece of valuable equipment! It was the centurion, not the servant, that everyone felt sorry for! Are you ever tempted to regard some people almost as 'things', or as means to ends? Might Jesus be wanting to rescue these people too? How can you put yourself in a position for that to happen?

Thinking back

9. How can we strengthen our faith so that it is more like that shown by the centurion? Make your answers the basis for prayer.

Going further

10. In the book of Acts, Luke's sequel to his gospel, more and more non-Jews like the centurion appear. Look at Luke 23:45–48 and Acts 1:1–8. Jesus speaks of the good news going to the non-Jewish world. He points out that the Scriptures (the Old Testament) speak of the good news being for all nations, and prophesies that it will go throughout the world after his death and resurrection. How important is such a vision of world mission to you? For the distinction between 'Jew' and 'non-Jew', try reading 'people familiar to you in your culture' and 'those of alien cultures'.

Memory verse
Luke 7:9: 'I tell you, I have not found such great faith even in Israel.'

Dr Luke and his gospel

As a Greek doctor, Luke is trained to listen carefully and pay attention to detail. He has a sharp eye for the sick, the socially handicapped, for children or for people who are 'different'. He is interested in the deeper causes of our human problems.

During an adventurous life he became a close friend of Paul, the famous early Christian leader and speaker. They walked, rode and sailed incredible distances together, even enduring stoning and prison. Paul speaks of him in his letter to the small church at Colosse as 'our dear friend Luke, the doctor' (Colossians 4:14).

Luke's gospel (the word means 'good news') was written for someone called Theophilus, about whom we know nothing. He may have been a Roman official Luke had met on his travels, but the book was also written for a wider audience, among whom you can now number yourself.

This is the first of a two-part work. The second instalment, known as the Acts of the Apostles, takes the story on another twenty years. It shows, through the story of the young church, how the good news – the 'big story' – spread out from Jerusalem to begin changing the Roman empire. Too many have dismissed Christianity without ever knowing what it is. Dr Luke's two short books are written to overcome that deficiency.

It helps to know what type (or genre) a book is in order to understand it. If you like science-fiction stories, you can go to a science-fiction and fantasy section of a bookshop and be reasonably certain of finding a book to meet your expectations there. Similarly, you might go to a biography or a computing section for very different types of books.

Luke's type of book is a 'gospel', like three other New Testament books by Matthew, Mark and John. John's is the most different of the four, but recognizably belongs to the category. Gospels are quite like biographies and histories. There is no first-century type of literature to which the gospels naturally belong, however. It is clear that the world-changing events they record forced the creation of a new form or type of book. The existence of the gospels is in itself a dramatic evidence of the truth and reality of the Christian message. The gospels emerge, unique, in the first-century world.

The gospels have all the features of the greatest stories told by human beings, including the most astounding of sudden, happy endings (J. R. R. Tolkien called such endings *eucatastrophe*). What is different is that the gospels are not simply myth, or legend; they are not human tales of the involvement of gods and supernatural beings in human affairs. The radical and unique feature of the gospels is that the historical facts themselves are the greatest story. God has ordered the events, as it were, in the manner of a master story-teller, but dealing with history rather than a fictional world. The events are witnessed by reliable people whose accounts are the bedrock of the gospels, as Luke makes clear in his introduction.

Jesus and social misfits

Luke 7:11–17, 36–50

If you think society today stacks the odds against people who are physically, socially or economically disadvantaged, imagine how much worse it was in Jesus' day. No social security . . . no social services . . . only the most rudimentary medical care . . . no equal-rights legislation, and few opportunities for education, training and rehabilitation. Women were particularly hard-hit. (Luke shows particular interest in their needs and their part in the story of Jesus.) On top of that, those who suffered were despised by the able-bodied and better-off – rather as the prosperous sometimes despise the 'underclass' today. It was their own fault, wasn't it? They must have done *something* to forfeit God's blessing!

Last time we looked at the faith of the centurion, a non-Jew. This study looks at two other occasions when Jesus rescued people who were, in one way or another, misfits in society. We've already seen that this is one of the main things Luke emphasizes about Jesus. No-one is too near the bottom of the heap, no situation too hopeless, to be beyond the reach of Jesus' power to deliver. 'The blind receive sight, the lame walk, those who have leprosy are cured, the deaf hear, the dead are raised, and the good news is preached to the poor' (7:22).

Opening up

1. Think of some 'problem' situations' you know. Your friend whose childhood traumas left her emotionally wrecked;

your stressed-out relative sinking into alcoholism; the fellow on your course who's in a mess because of the lifestyle he chose . . . can Jesus really deliver them? Your theologically correct head says yes, but what do you really believe in your guts?

Look at several newspapers (tabloids and broadsheets) to find evidence of human 'wrecks' in the news. They might be victims of injustice or political oppression, or they might display obvious moral failings or emotional needs.

Exploring the story

Read Luke 7:11–17

2. Imagine the widow's plight. She will have been dependent on her son's earning-power. Now she was not only doubly bereaved but reduced to destitution too. What was Jesus' instinctive reaction?

Verse 13. Of the gospel writers, Luke is alone in frequently describing Jesus as 'the Lord'. Except in Mark 11:3 it is not usually used of Jesus during his life on earth. When people did address Jesus directly as 'Lord' (see Luke 5:8; 7:6), this was usually simply an equivalent of 'sir' – a common term of respect.

3. The act of touching the open coffin made Jesus ritually unclean according to the Jewish religious laws. How far would you risk your 'religious respectability' in order to respond in compassion to someone in need? Do you think Jesus even thought about it?

4. As in the case of the centurion and his servant (study 5), Jesus delivered two people by healing one of them. In this case, the son had actually died, and you can't get a more hopeless situation than that! How has this story encouraged you to believe that Jesus can rescue the 'impossible' people you thought about in question 1?

Read Luke 7:36–50

5. He was a man and a Pharisee; she a mere woman, and a prostitute at that. Which of them would Jesus' society have considered the more likely to be 'saved' (accepted by God)? Which actually was saved? What made the difference?

6. How did Simon and the woman express their different attitudes to Jesus? What do you think was going on in the woman when she acted as she did?

7. Again, Jesus was made ritually unclean, this time by physical contact with the 'unclean' woman. How did Simon view her 'touching' of Jesus? How did Jesus view it?

8. What point does Jesus make to Simon in his story about the two debtors? Have you seen the same pattern in people who have become Christians? Can you believe that it can happen again in the lives of the people you thought about in question 1?

Thinking back

9. Quietly meditate on what your own 'perfume' of love and repentance could be.

10. Reflect on the people you may, deep down, consider in some way 'unclean', and to be avoided, especially people you might encounter in your daily life. How comfortable would your church be if such people (say, alcoholics, down-and-outs, people with learning difficulties) came to a service? How comfortable would those people be in the service? How can you improve matters?

Going further

11. This session has focused on two very different women in a very male-oriented culture. How would you describe Jesus' attitude to them? What attitudes did he *not* display to them? How might all this help you to respond to someone who felt that Christianity oppresses women?

Memory verse

Luke 7:50: 'Jesus said to the woman, "Your faith has saved you; go in peace."'

Salvation

Salvation is a marvellously rich word which Luke uses in describing the extraordinary ministry of Jesus. The word he uses for 'save' (the Greek word *sozō*) can also mean 'heal' – which may help to explain Luke the doctor's special interest.

For Luke, salvation focuses on the person of Jesus Christ. After the birth of John the Baptist, his father Zechariah prophesies and concentrates on the salvation for which he will pave the way (1:68–79). Announcing the birth of Jesus, the angel tells the shepherds, 'Today in the town of David a *Saviour* has been born to you' (2:11). When Joseph and Mary take him to the temple in Jerusalem, they are met by Simeon, an old man who 'was waiting for the consolation of Israel' (2:25). He takes Jesus in his arms and praises God: 'My eyes have seen your *salvation*, which you have prepared in the sight of all people (2:30–31).

Luke sees Jesus as the culmination of God's plan of salvation which has been gathering pace throughout history. He draws attention to the way Jesus fulfils what was predicted hundreds of years previously by the Old Testament prophets (see 3:4–6; 4:18–21; 10:23–24; 24:26–27, 44–47) and is careful to emphasize that Jesus is the Saviour, not merely of Israel, but of the whole world: 'All mankind shall see God's salvation' (3:6). All this forms the background for what Peter says about Jesus in Acts 4:12: 'Salvation is found in no-one else, for there is no other name under heaven given to men by which we must be saved'.

That's all very well, but what does the world need to be saved *from*? At one level, Luke recounts how the ministry of Jesus brought rescue from the evil trio of disease, demons and death (examples of all three are found in chapter 8, for example). When Jesus is on the cross, this is the aspect that the bystanders focus on as they jeer, 'He saved others; let him save himself' (23:35–39).

But salvation means much more than this. One of the key passages in Luke's gospel is 5:31–32, where Jesus declares, 'It is not the healthy who need a doctor, but the sick. I have not come to call the righteous, but sinners to repentance.' Jesus taught that the deepest and most basic need shared by all humanity is to be saved from the consequences of our sin, our self-centred rebellion against God. Being saved is not just about being freed from the problems we have with our minds and bodies. It has a spiritual dimension as well. To be completely whole we need to be forgiven, put right with God and with one another.

The story of Zacchaeus the cheating tax official is a good example. His encounter with Jesus leads him to want to put things right by giving away half his possessions and paying back those he had cheated four times the amount he had stolen. In response to his declaration to this effect Jesus is able to say, 'Today salvation has come to this house, because this man, too, is a son of Abraham. For the Son of Man came to seek and to save what was lost' (19:9–10). There was nothing *physically* wrong with Zacchaeus. What he needed was to be made whole *spiritually*.

So Jesus came that people might have 'knowledge of salvation by the forgiveness of their sins' (1:77). He did this by allowing himself to be crucified, refusing to save himself (as he could so easily have done) but choosing instead to save others (23:35–43) in a far deeper sense than those present realized. After his resurrection he explained to his disciples that he was simply fulfilling what the Old Testament had predicted – that he would 'suffer and rise from the dead on the third day, and repentance and forgiveness of sins will be preached in his name to all nations' (24:46–47). The implication is clear: repentance and forgiveness of sins are now possible because of his sufferings and resurrection.

How does salvation come about? Several times Luke makes the link between salvation and faith. Jesus tells several of those who come to him for healing that their faith has saved them, or will do so (see 7:50; 8:48, 50; 17:19; 18:42). In the parable of the sower the devil is shown to be intent on taking away the word of God from people's hearts, 'so that they may not believe and be saved' (8:12).

Such belief is more than mere intellectual assent: it includes the vital element of trust, to the point of letting go of the things of this life which we can see in favour of the things of the life to come which we cannot see. As Jesus said, 'If anyone would come after me, he must deny himself and take up his cross daily and follow me. For whoever wants to save his life will lose it, but whoever loses his life for me will save it. What good is it for a man to gain the whole world, and yet lose or forfeit his very self?' (9:23–25).

Salvation is God's free gift, but it's so big that we have to drop everything else to keep hold of it. No wonder then that Jesus is asked, 'Lord, are only a few people going to be saved?' (13:23).

Later on, salvation is also seen in terms of entering the kingdom of God (18:25–26). As Jesus sets out the stringent terms involved, the response is, 'Who then can be saved?' His answer holds out hope to all: 'What is impossible with men is possible with God.'

Among the crowds

Luke 6:17–49; 9:10–17

Which are you – a crowd-lover ('The more the merrier') or a crowd-hater ('Oh for some peace and quiet – and some space!')? Jesus, as a celebrity, had to cope with crowds. As we shall see in these passages, that meant dealing with

●   the needs of the crowd as a whole
●   the needs of individuals within the crowd
●   his disciples' needs amid the crowd
●   his own needs amid the crowd

En route, we'll take in a good chunk of his teaching – much of it about relationships.

Opening up

1. As we've hinted, different personality types react differently to crowds. Think about your own strengths in relation to different kinds of Christian involvement. Are you more comfortable taking part in a big, public event, or in a small group or one-to-one friendship? Are you happier in a teaching role or a practical one? Jesus demonstrated God's love for people in *all* these ways – so don't feel inferior if you're not a Steve Chalke!

Divide a sheet of paper into two columns headed 'Strengths' and 'Weaknesses', and then list your strengths and weaknesses in respect of (a) your church involvement, and (b) the ways you express your faith in your everyday life and work.

Exploring the story

Read Luke 6:17–19

2. Try to picture the scene. How would you feel if all those people were making all those demands on you? Do you sometimes feel that other people's needs are draining you? We're not Jesus! – but how can we cope?

Read Luke 6:20–26

3. Despite all the practical healing ministry that Jesus had been so busy with, he made it a priority to give his disciples the teaching they needed. How can we balance attending to people's pressing, practical needs with ministering to their more 'spiritual' needs? Do we make enough time ourselves to receive teaching (through Bible study, books, sermons, housegroups, *etc.*)?

4. This famous passage is about extreme contrasts between the conditions of people now and in the future. What words would you use to describe Jesus' teaching here? Which 'beatitudes' particularly challenge you?

Read Luke 6:27–36

5. Do you think Jesus is asking too much? In verses 35–36, what motivation does he set before us?

Read Luke 6:37–42

6. What are the cons of a critical attitude to others, and the pros of a generous one? How do you match up?

Read Luke 6:43–45

7. When we're under pressure, we often reveal what's inside us – the attitudes we can bottle up when life is relatively easy for us. When people know you, what splashes out? How can the 'overflow' be made sweeter?

Read Luke 6:46–49

8. At the end of this section of teaching, Jesus emphasizes that just hearing it (or reading it) is not enough. How can we ensure that our foundations as Christians will stand up to the torrents when they strike?

Read Luke 9:10–17

9. Jesus felt the need to withdraw with his closest friends – but he wasn't allowed any respite from the crowds. How did he react? At other times he *did* manage to get away to rest and pray. How can we ensure that we give due attention to our own needs while not seeming to push away other people who need us?

10. Why do you think Jesus involved his disciples in a 'team effort' to meet the crowd's 'impossible' needs? What can we learn from this?

> Verse 16. It is possible that Jesus used the Jewish grace, 'Blessed are you, O Lord our God, King of the world, who brings forth bread from the earth.'

Thinking back

11. Go back to the last part of question 9, thinking of it in the larger terms of what you have considered in this session. If you feel 'crowded out' by the needs and demands of others, reflect on Christ's perhaps surprising offer of a reward in verse 35.

Going further

12. Look at the list of Jesus' parables in the following section. Try to read through all of these in the next few days in the light of the section. From time to time, have a go at putting a parable into a modern setting, as suggested.

Memory verses

Luke 6:35–36: 'But love your enemies, do good to them, and lend to them without expecting to get anything back. Then your reward will be great, and you will be sons of the Most High, because he is kind to the ungrateful and wicked. Be merciful, just as your Father is merciful.'

The parables of Jesus

Much of the teaching of Jesus which Luke records in his gospel is in the form of parables. 'Parable' is a word whose root suggests the idea of making an abstract truth easier to understand by setting it alongside and likening it to something more concrete and down to earth.

We tend to connect parables particularly with Jesus. But this isn't a form of teaching that he invented. Plenty of others had used it before. Indeed, the Old Testament book we call 'Proverbs' could equally well be translated 'Parables'; the Hebrew word is the same. Even so, it's clear that whereas other teachers would use a parable to illustrate something they were trying to get across, Jesus used the parables *themselves* to convey the whole of what he wanted to say, especially when talking to the crowds. They would be left with memorable stories to think about. This is what marks out Jesus as such a skilled communicator to ordinary people. No wonder they enjoyed listening to him!

We also tend to think of the parables as 'stories'. But this isn't quite right. Even the gospels themselves apply the label 'parable' to other sorts of picture language as well. Here are two examples in Luke.

Luke 5:36. He told them this parable: 'No-one tears a patch from a new garment and sews it on an old one. If he does, he will have torn the new garment, and the patch from the new will not match the old.'

Luke 6:39. He also told them this parable: 'Can a blind man lead a blind man? Will they not both fall into a pit?'

Not much of a story in these two cases! And yet they're still parables. On this basis, Luke includes as many as forty-five of them in his gospel. Here's a list of them, together with a note of whether or not they are also found in Matthew (Mt) and Mark (Mk):

5:31–32	Mt Mk	Doctor to the sick
5:33–39	Mt Mk	The bridegroom's guests
5:36	Mt Mk	The unshrunk cloth
5:37–39	Mt Mk	The new wine
6:39	Mt	Blind guides
6:41–42	Mt	The plank and the speck
6:43–45	Mt	Bad trees
6:47–49	Mt	The two houses
7:31–35	Mt	The children playing
7:41–50	Lk alone	The two debtors
8:4–8, 11–15	Mt Mk	The sower
8:16–18	Mt Mk	The lamp
10:25–37	Lk alone	The good Samaritan
11:5–8	Lk alone	The friend at midnight
11:11–13	Mt	The father and his children's requests
11:14–20	Mt Mk	The divided kingdom and house
11:21–23	Mt Mk	The strong man bound
11:24–26	Mt	The return of the evil spirit
11:33–36	Mt	The lamp
12:13–21	Lk alone	The rich fool
12:32–34	Mt	Laying up treasure in heaven
12:35–38	Mt Mk	The watchmen
12:39–40	Mt	The thief
12:42–46	Mt	The steward
12:57–59	Mt	Going to court
13:6–9	Lk alone	The fig tree

13:18–19	Mt Mk	The mustard seed
13:20–21	Mt	The leaven
13:23–27	Mt	The door
14:7–14	Lk alone	Places at table
14:16–24	Mt	The great feast
14:28–30	Lk alone	The tower-builder
14:31–33	Lk alone	The king going to war
14:34–35	Mt Mk	Salt
15:1–7	Mt	The lost sheep
15:8–10	Lk alone	The lost coin
15:11–32	Lk alone	The lost son
16:1–13	Lk alone	The unjust steward
16:19–31	Lk alone	The rich man and Lazarus
17:7–10	Lk alone	The humble servant
18:1–8	Lk alone	The unjust judge
18:9–14	Lk alone	The Pharisee and the tax-collector
19:11–27	Mt	The talents and the pounds
20:9–19	Mt Mk	The wicked tenants
21:29–33	Mt Mk	The budding fig tree

There's considerable overlap, but fifteen of them are unique to Luke. Whereas Matthew concentrates on stories that illustrate the nature of the kingdom of God, Luke tends to select stories about the activities of ordinary people in day-to-day situations. They bring out what Jesus had to say about money and possessions, pride and humility, and the need to count the cost before beginning to follow him. Others give a unique insight into God's character as the one who delights to seek out the lost and welcome in the outsider.

We should also note that as well as telling parables, Jesus also *did* them. Many of his actions, especially his miracles of healing, had symbolic significance and communicated his message of salvation powerfully. Perhaps the most moving of these is his action in giving the broken bread and the wine to his disciples on the night before his body was to be broken and his blood shed on the cross.

Although Jesus used parables to *reveal* truth and bring it home to his listeners, the gospels also record that Jesus taught in this way in order to *conceal* the truth of what he was saying. Before responding to his disciples' request to tell them what the parable of the sower meant, Jesus said this: 'The knowledge of the secrets of the kingdom of God has been given to you, but to others I speak in parables, so that, "though seeing, they may not see; though hearing, they may not understand"' (Luke 8:10; the quotation is from Isaiah 6:9).

Parables thus have a dual function. They communicate truth about God only to those who have been given the spiritual ability to understand their deeper meaning. These are those who, like the disciples, are serious about trusting and obeying Jesus. On the other hand, parables serve to obscure the truth to those who refuse to believe and apply what Jesus says to their own lives. Such people are satisfied with the surface impact of a good story.

Although much of what the parables contain is timeless, it can sometimes be helpful to 'translate' the details into our own culture in order to experience more of the impact they would have had when Jesus first told them. For example, instead of the 'parable of the good Samaritan', read it through as the 'parable of the good terrorist'.

Jesus and religious people

Luke 14:1–24

How do we become Christians? Do we become acceptable to God by being 'religious' – by obeying certain rules and regulations or taking part in ceremonies? Or is it our social status or membership of some religious 'club' that makes us Christians? Lots of people think that their religious practice, social status, or even nationality, means that they are OK with God. Many believe that being religious makes you a better person.

Jesus encountered a wide variety of religious people; some, like Zechariah (Luke 1), Simeon and Anna (Luke 2), recognized him as the Messiah. And some, like the Jews in the synagogue in Luke 4, did not. In the end the religious authorities of the day became the primary human agency that secured Jesus' crucifixion. In this story we find Jesus at a dinner party arranged by one of the leading Jewish religious leaders.

Jesus is no stranger to controversy with the religious leaders of his day. The passage gives us helpful insight into how religious rules, status, power and tradition can in fact be a bar to knowing God. It is possible that the comment by a guest in verse 15 was made on the assumption that the guest will automatically be at the heavenly banquet. Jesus then goes on to illustrate that those who were originally invited to come into the kingdom would lose their places to others who, in the world's eyes, were less deserving.

Whether all the events in the passage happened at the same meal, or are merely grouped together by Luke for our instruction, has no real implications for the essential messages of the passage.

Opening up

1. Someone interviewing you for a job would pay close attention to your qualifications, background and education. The interviewer might rely on what your previous employer says about you. On which basis does God decide whether or not we are fit to serve him? List the qualities you might put in your *c.v.* and which might help you get the job if God were your prospective employer.

Exploring the story

Read Luke 14:1–24

2. Try to summarize the main theme(s) underlying Jesus' teaching in the passage.

Read verses 1–6

3. What do you think were the motives of the prominent Pharisee (verse 1) when he invited Jesus to the meal?

4. According to the rules set down by the leading religious teachers of the day, it was not lawful to heal on the Sabbath unless there was an immediate danger to life. Why do you think that the Pharisees and experts in religious law were unable (or unwilling?) to answer Jesus' question in verse 5?

Verse 2: The term 'dropsy' refers to a medical condition in which the body tends to swell with fluid. For an explanation of 'experts in the law', see the Word List entry on 'Scribes'.

---

5. Sometimes churches or Christian groups set certain standards of behaviour – what is and is not acceptable for a Christian to do. These rules and regulations often have no real basis in Scripture; instead, they are based on attitudes and values from many sources. Think of any such attitudes, values, rules or regulations that you are familiar with. In what ways might these have the effect of discouraging Christians from behaving as Christ would have done? (See 'Keeping the Rules', p. 78.)

Read verses 7–11

6. Some of the guests might have been flattered by an invitation to eat in the house of such a prominent Pharisee. It may have made them feel important. Jesus instead instructed the guests to be genuinely humble. How might Jesus' words have challenged their ideas about their relationship with God?

Read verses 12–14

7. At the heart of the world's idea of religion is the attitude that says: 'If I do this for God he will bless me' – just as we might think, 'If I do this for her, she will like me.' Which qualities does Jesus encourage his host to demonstrate?

8. You can probably think of several people who wouldn't be in a position to 'repay' you for kindness. In what practical ways can you demonstrate love to such people?

The parable of the great banquet (verses 15–24) is a picture of God's offer of salvation to human beings. To those who accept his free gift, there is an intimate relationship with God. They will enjoy his presence and all that he gives them. The parable emphasizes that God's invitation is not accepted by those who consider themselves fine as they are. Instead, those with no status or influence in the world's eyes are the ones who accept the invitation. There is a similar story in Matthew 22:1–14.

It is unlikely that someone would have bought a field without first inspecting it (verse 18). No-one would sensibly have bought oxen (verse 19) without first checking that they were not lame. The excuse in verse 20 is probably drawn from the advice in Deuteronomy 24:5, which excuses a newly married man from military service. But this instruction was not intended to remove him from social contact (see Leon Morris, *Luke*, p. 234), but rather to provide an opportunity for the couple's marital relationship to be firmly established. What appears to have been behind the excuses was a preoccupation with the here and now; in essence the idolatry of things and relationships. Jesus' hearers would have found the excuses amusing, probably until they realized that they themselves were being described. The religious elite were too busy with their daily preoccupation of obeying religious rules, maintaining their status and exercising their ecclesiastical power. Therefore their invitations were handed out to those in the town who they regarded as 'inferior'. After that, the invitations went to people beyond the town – presumably a reference to the Gentiles.

9. Note the urgency with which the slave is sent out to offer the invitation. Do we evangelize with the same urgency?

10. Try to imagine your reactions to what Jesus said if you were one of the Pharisees or experts in the law listening to Jesus' teaching. Why would you have reacted in this way?

Thinking back

11. Spend some time praying about some of the practical ideas that you have picked up from this session's passage. It will help you to identify particular attitudes of which you have become aware and which you need to bring before Christ. You may wish to pray in silence, or together as a group.

Going further

12. In Luke 11:37–54, Jesus pronounces six woes against the religious leaders, like an Old Testament prophet. This reinforced their opposition to him (ultimately leading to his execution). Why does Jesus use such invective? To what extent are you 'religious' rather than a human person being transformed by God's grace? Do you try to change only the outside of yourself, or are you changing from the inside? Where does change really come from?

Memory verse

Luke 14:11: 'For everyone who exalts himself will be humbled, and he who humbles himself will be exalted.'

Keeping the rules

In the pages of Luke's gospel, Jesus clashes with religious leaders who imposed rigid ethical codes. Churches or groups, sometimes with the best intentions, often set up unwritten rules or codes of behaviour which you have to obey in order to be acceptable to the group. They might cover issues such as standards of dress, which version of the Bible you use, whether you can engage in certain leisure activities or your view on certain matters of biblical interpretation.

These rules or codes of behaviour may reflect deep-seated attitudes and values, which are often worldly, not scriptural. They are often a cultural by-product (for instance, in England, Anglo-Saxon reluctance to discuss money may limit the effectiveness of English Christians' stewardship of money). Rules also give those who make them power over those who are supposed to obey them.

The key issue in examining such rules is: 'In the light of Scripture, are they justifiable?' While the rules were designed to help spiritual growth, they often have the effect of making us subject to legalism. The essential concern becomes outward behaviour and conformity to the expected standards rather than inward attitudes. Ultimately they exclude people: 'If you don't do this, think that or believe the other, you are not a proper Christian.'

Jesus and his captors

Luke 22:39–71

Having shared his last meal with the twelve disciples, the climax of Christ's mission begins to draw near. Those who had been hostile to him from the early days of his ministry now move in for the kill. This passage tells the story of Jesus' arrest and the formal part of his trial before the Jewish authorities.

In contrast to how Hollywood might have written the script, Jesus does not call upon reserves of strength or armies of angels to destroy those who try to arrest him. Instead he goes through with the arrest, which takes him ultimately to the cross.

Luke tells us that for a long time the Jewish authorities have been looking for an opportunity to arrest and discredit Jesus – see for example Luke 19:47–48; 20:26. Judas, now under the control of the devil (Luke 22:3), goes to the Jewish authorities and offers to betray Jesus. (This is presumably to arrange to identify him so that he can be arrested.) Luke 22:7–38 describes the events of the last supper, where Jesus warns the Twelve of both his impending betrayal and his consequent death. The disciples seem strangely unaware of what is about to befall Jesus and the temptations that are about to overwhelm them: their conversation over dinner is about which of them would be considered to be the greatest.

Jesus knew from early in his life that the world would make a cross for him; indeed that would fulfil biblical prophecy. Behind the human agency – the Jewish and Roman authorities who tried, convicted and crucified him – was of course the devil, out to destroy God's Son and divert Jesus from his mission to save humankind.

Jesus' reaction to his friends who betrayed or denied him, and to his captors, demonstrated not only his perfect composure under the extreme pressure of the spiritual battle, but also his readiness to suffer rejection as part of the cost of the cross.

Opening up

1. Which of Jesus' disciples do you most identify with? Imagine that you are one of the disciples. From what you have learned over the last few sessions, what do you expect Jesus to achieve in Jerusalem?

Exploring the story

Read Luke 22:39–71

2. Looking at all the events in the passage, what strikes you most about the attitude(s) of Jesus towards both his friends who betrayed or denied him, and those who captured and tried him?

3. The apostle John tells us that Jesus came to 'destroy the devil's work' (1 John 3:8). What evidence is there in the passage to suggest that the disciples did not understand the nature of the spiritual battle that Christ was engaged in?

This passage graphically illustrates some aspects of the spiritual battle ('the darkness' in verse 53):

● the conflict Christ felt in the garden in prayer, as he faced the prospect of taking our sin upon himself and thereby experiencing separation from God (verses 42–44);

● the betrayal by Judas who ensured that the authorities arrested the right person (verse 48). Note also his inability to repent or feel remorse, in contrast to Peter's reaction on the realization of his denial (verse 62);

● the temptation of the disciples to fight spiritual battles with earthly weapons (verses 46, 50);

● the underhand way they arrested Jesus at night (verses 52–53); and

● the spiritual blindness of the Jewish leaders who were sending to death the very Messiah they longed for (verses 67–71). (Luke 23:50–51 tells us that not all the Jewish leaders consented, however.)

Read verses 39–46

4. How can Jesus' teaching and example in these verses help you pray?

5. If you were a police officer going to arrest a group of criminals, it would be surprising if one of the criminals helped you in the arrest – let alone healed you of an injury you sustained during it! What impression do you think that Jesus' healing of the servant's ear left on the servant and all those watching?

6. Verse 39 says that Jesus behaved as normal by going to the Mount of Olives on the night he was to be arrested. He also refused to protect himself and made no attempt to resist arrest. What does Jesus' behaviour tell us about his understanding of what his captors were doing in the light of what he knew of God's plan?

7. Have you ever felt tempted to deny Christ? Suggest the conflicts and loyalties one might feel in such a situation.

8. What impression do you think that Peter's denial of Christ made upon those watching?

The trial procedure to which Christ was subjected was highly irregular. Under their own law the Jews falsely convicted Christ of blasphemy, an offence punishable by death. But, being an occupied state, they had no power to execute without the approval of the Romans. Blasphemy of the Jewish God was not really something the pagan Roman government was worried about. So the Jews got Jesus tried by the Romans on charges of sedition in allegedly refusing to pay taxes, and in claiming to be King of the Jews. Luke 22 records the formal part of Jesus' trial before the Jewish supreme court, the Sanhedrin (or Council), held the morning after Jesus' arrest. The different elements of Jesus' trial before the Jews were as follows:

●   Immediately after his arrest Jesus is first interviewed during the night by Annas, a former high priest (John 18:12–14) and then by the current high priest Caiaphas and the Council (Mark 14:53–64).

●   Presumably to regularize the decision made informally during the night, the Council meets at daybreak and finds Jesus guilty (Luke 22:66–71).

Jesus is then sent for trial to the Roman authorities (Luke 23:1 onwards. See the Word List entry on the *Sanhedrin*.)

9. Why do you think that the Jewish leaders wanted Jesus dead?

> The use of the term 'prophesy' (verse 64) can be explained by the belief that prophets in the first century were usually thought able to predict the future and explain mysteries. The soldiers therefore put this 'prophet' to the test as if he were a fortune-teller or fairground psychic.

Read verses 66–71

10. Analyse the answers Jesus gave – or did not give – to the questions he was posed. Why do you think he responded in the way that he did?

Thinking back

11. Meditate on the implications of Jesus' submission to God's will. He did not find this easy, and he was deliberately led into suffering. We know the whole story and its glorious ending. We may be in a story unfolding right now in our lives, however, where we do not yet know the ending and where following

God's will is going to be far from easy. What kept Jesus' eyes firmly on the road ahead?

Going further

12. Read through Luke's carefully documented account of Christ's death and burial in Luke 23. Imagine that you are an onlooker and a follower of Jesus. You don't yet know the magnificent happy ending, even though the Old Testament speaks of it. Think of the doubts and confusion which would rack you as your leader dies, the victim of evil and injustice. You would not sleep that night. You might be asking where God was in all this.

Carefully go through some of the reasons Jesus had to die (see the following section).

Memory verse
Luke 22:42: 'Father, if you are willing, take this cup from me; yet not my will, but yours be done.'

Why did Jesus have to die?

The apostles who followed Jesus explained the vital importance of his death in many different ways.

- He paid the price to ransom us (1 Timothy 2:6).
- He carried our sins (1 Peter 2:24).
- He experienced the curse that we deserve (Galatians 3:13).
- He offered a sacrifice for the world's sin (Hebrews 10:12).
- He died for our sins (1 Corinthians 15:3).

What all the word-pictures combine to make clear is that the death of one man nineteen centuries ago (by a method that was horribly familiar at the time) has a permanent effect throughout the centuries on our relationship with God. Without it there would be an immovable barrier between mankind and God.

No Messiah that Jews could recognize could suffer such a death: for 'a hanged man is accursed by God' (Deuteronomy 21:23, RSV). 'An insult to God'; so says an ancient Jewish 'Targum' (a religious tract).

That in fact was exactly the problem that Saul of Tarsus, arch-persecutor of the early church, wrestled with before his conversion. He knew the grim Old Testament law which decreed that a criminal's body should be suspended from a tree or pole after execution. It demonstrated that sentence had been carried out. The law stated, 'Anyone who is hung on a tree is under God's curse' (this didn't mean that God curses someone *because* he was hanged, but that he was hanged because he had already been 'cursed' *i.e.* condemned and offered up for punishment).

Since Jesus' crucifixion was technically 'hanging from a tree', the very suggestion that he could be the promised deliverer from God would horrify any Jew. How can *he* be God's Son, when he seems to bear God's curse?

Paul shares the secret that eventually broke upon his own astonished understanding. Yes – Jesus was experiencing the curse. But it was not his – it was ours. He endured the awful sense of being condemned and banished from God – not for any misdeeds of his own (he had none) but for our misdeeds, for which he took the responsibility.

So Paul writes: 'All who rely on observing the law are under a curse, for it is written: "Cursed is everyone who does not continue to do everything written in the Book of the Law" . . . Christ redeemed us from the curse of the law by becoming a curse for us, for it is written, "Cursed is everyone who is hung on a tree"' (Galatians 3:10–13).

Some parallels

Dying for someone else is not unknown in human experience. Captain Oates walked into the blizzard to give his companions a chance to escape in Scott's expedition of 1912. A concentration-camp inmate takes the place of the chosen victim.

Paying for someone else happens too: a parent pays a heavy fine for his child's crime, a research scientist drives himself to breakdown in order to perfect a cure.

All this and much more Jesus did on a cosmic scale at his crucifixion.

The risen Jesus and his friends

Luke 24:13–44

What is the greatest miracle in the Bible? Is it one of Jesus' healings or the feeding of the five thousand? Or that God came to earth as a human at all? There is probably no simple answer to the question! But on any basis someone being raised from the dead is pretty remarkable. However much the resurrection of Jesus verges on the unbelievable to the western twentieth-century mind, it is utterly central to the Christian faith. As Paul, one of the major contributors to the New Testament, put it: 'And if Christ has not been raised, our preaching is useless and so is your faith . . . your faith is futile . . . you are still in your sins' (1 Corinthians 15:14,17).

But even the disciples, initially, did not believe the evidence for the resurrection. Here we meet Jesus proving to his friends that he had indeed risen from the dead.

Matthew 27:62 – 28:4 tells us that the authorities were so worried that the disciples might steal the body and pretend that Jesus had risen that they specially sealed the tomb and posted guards to prevent it happening. God sent an angel to open the tomb, the effect of which (along with an earthquake!) was to terrify the guards.

Luke 24 then takes up the story of the discovery by the friends of Jesus that he has risen from the dead. First a group of women go to the tomb, only to be told by angels that Jesus is risen. Given that the testimony of women was not acceptable in a Jewish court, it is a notable challenge to cultural attitudes and stereotypes that God announces it to the women first. Secondly, Peter and company (disbelieving the women) go to the tomb themselves to check. The disciples must have been acutely demoralized; to find that the body had disappeared must have been almost the last straw – given that the reality of Jesus' promise to rise from the dead had not sunk in. This passage is Luke's record of some of Jesus' post-resurrection appearances to his friends.

Opening up

1. What is your experience of niggling doubts about the truth and reality of Christian faith? How important is the fact of Jesus' resurrection going to be in overcoming such reservations?

Exploring the story

Read Luke 24:13–44

2. Summarize the evidence in this passage for Jesus' physical resurrection from the dead.

3. Look at what the passage tells us about the state of mind of the two disciples on the road to Emmaus. Why did they feel as they did?

4. Verse 16 implies that the two disciples were prevented from recognizing Jesus at first. Why do you think Christ initially concealed his identity from them?

5. The two disciples described Jesus as a 'prophet' (verse 19), as opposed to 'the Messiah'. Describe the practical implications of believing that Jesus was merely a prophet, instead of being the Messiah. (For an explanation of *Messiah* and *Prophet* see the Word List).

6. The two disciples expected Jesus to 'redeem Israel' (verse 21). From the conversations between Jesus and the groups of disciples, how does he challenge their understanding of what he had come to do?

Verse 21: '*Redeem*' generally refers to something being bought back on the payment of a price. When used in terms of Christ's death on the cross, the meaning is modified from its traditional usage in that God does not have to pay anyone anything in order to set us free. In the New Testament *redeem* means the act of Christ setting us free from sin by taking our place on the cross. The two disciples may have thought only in terms of Jesus liberating Israel from the Roman rule, so his dying at the hands of the authorities would have represented failure.

7. What aspects of Jesus' character are shown to us by the way he deals with the disciples' doubts throughout the passage?

8. A number of people down the ages have claimed to be the Messiah. How did the disciples know that the person before them was the authentic Christ?

Thinking back

9. How would you explain the significance of Jesus' death and resurrection to a non-Christian?

10. The disciples both knew the truth about Jesus from Scripture (verses 27, 44) and personally encountered him risen from the dead (verses 31–32, 36). Why is the right balance between Scripture and experience important in our daily Christian living and in our evangelism?

Going further

11. Read right through Luke 24 making a note of the realness of Jesus' presence. (See the following article.) Note the characteristics of his physical reality – his 'touchableness', his scars, his digestive system (he ate), his rationality, his understanding of the disciples' fears. Note also the aspects which show that Jesus is part of a new creation – his ability to appear and disappear. Why is it so important that Jesus isn't merely a ghost (verse 39)? Why does Luke record so much evidence for Jesus' resurrection?

Memory verse
Luke 24:27: 'And beginning with Moses and all the Prophets, he explained to them what was said in all the Scriptures concerning himself.'

The resurrection of Jesus

The resurrection of Jesus from the dead is the key to the truth of Christianity. If it did not happen and the corpse remains buried somewhere in Jerusalem, then we are wasting our time with an illusion – comforting, maybe, but ultimately hollow. As Paul puts it in 1 Corinthians 15:14, 'if Christ has not been raised, our preaching is useless and so is your faith'. On the other hand, if Christ *has* indeed been raised, then everything else slots into place. His victory over sin, death and the devil is assured.

Like the other gospel writers, Luke provides us with evidence to sustain the claim. He outlines the circumstances of Jesus' death and burial and describes the way in which the followers of Jesus reacted to the news of his empty tomb and then met him for themselves.

Of special significance to Luke is the physical reality of Jesus' resurrection body. He describes the impact made by Jesus during one of his appearances to his disciples: 'They were startled and frightened, thinking they saw a ghost. He said to them, "Why are you troubled, and why do doubts rise in your minds? Look at my hands and my feet. It is I myself! Touch me and see; a ghost does not have flesh and bones, as you see I have." When he had said this, he showed them his hands and feet. And while they still did not believe it because of joy and amazement, he asked them, "Do you have anything here to eat?" They gave him a piece of broiled fish, and he took it and ate it in their presence' (Luke 24:37–43).

Luke also wants his readers to grasp the way in which the resurrection of Jesus fits into God's whole scheme of things. He quotes Jesus as foretelling his death and resurrection as events that 'must' take place (9:22). He draws attention to the way in which the disciples were reminded of what Jesus had said about this (24:6–8), and also stresses the way the resurrection is part of what the Old Testament Scriptures prophesy about the Messiah (24:26–27, 44–46). The resurrection is no sudden reaction by God to the crisis of his Son's crucifixion: the whole sequence has been planned from the start.

But, of course, Luke doesn't stop there. The truth of the resurrection plays a major part in what he writes about the activities of the early church in Acts. Indeed, it seems to have been the main focus of their message, as Luke reports in Acts 4:33: 'With great power the apostles continued to testify to the *resurrection of the Lord Jesus*, and much grace was upon them all.'

The constant emphasis is, first of all, that God brought it about (2:24, 32; 3:15; 4:10; 5:30; 10:40; 13:30; 17:31). In raising his Son from death, he has publicly vindicated the claims made by Jesus, not least his promise that he would one day return as judge of all the world (17:31).

Secondly, the apostles speak as those who witnessed it, in the sense of having personally met with Jesus for the six weeks or so before his ascension (2:32; 3:15; 4:33; 10:40; 13:30). As Luke stresses, it was during this time that Jesus 'showed himself to these men and gave many convincing proofs that he was alive' (Acts 1:3). Certainly, being a witness to the resurrection was one of the major qualifications for the shortlist of those to replace Judas (see Acts 1:22). Paul implies that it is a factor in 1 Corinthians 15:7–9. Being able to stand up and give personal testimony that Jesus had indeed been raised from the dead was an important part of what it was to be an apostle.

Thirdly, as in his gospel, Luke brings out the resurrection as an event which fulfilled prophecy. For example, he quotes Peter on the day of Pentecost: 'But he [David] was a prophet and knew that God had promised him on oath that he would place one of his descendants on his throne. Seeing what was ahead, he spoke of the resurrection of the Christ, that he was not abandoned to the grave, nor did his body see decay' (Acts 2:30–31).

Of course, not everyone found the idea of resurrection very easy to accept. It was one of the main issues that divided the Pharisees from another religious party, the Sadducees. Luke describes how this group approached Jesus with a question designed to undermine the concept of resurrection, but were decisively trounced (Luke 20:27–40). Paul was able to exploit this difference on one occasion by claiming, when testifying before the Sanhedrin, that the reason he was on trial was the resurrection. The Pharisees and Sadducees present immediately forgot Paul and laid into each other (Acts 23:6–10)!

Guidelines for leaders

How do you feel about leading your group? Looking forward to it? Or a bit apprehensive?

You wouldn't be alone if you felt nervous. When God asked Moses to lead his people Israel out of slavery in Egypt, Moses shrank back, stammering, 'O Lord, please send someone else to do it' (Exodus 4:13)! Yet God so equipped and strengthened him for the task that he became one of Israel's greatest-ever leaders.

Leading your group won't be too difficult if you follow the guidelines below. You don't need to be a professor of theology, or to have teaching experience. In fact, you'll find that the group members will supply the engine-power for your discussions; all you need to do is a bit of steering along a well-signposted route. Once you get going, you'll enjoy it and find it rewarding.

Before you meet

1. Pray for the whole group, asking God to help each of you hear his Word during the session. Pray that you will all be motivated and guided to find ways of putting into practice what you learn. Pray that you will be built up together as a group and that the session will help people with any particular needs they may have.

2. Read the passage several times carefully and prayerfully. Try to imagine the scene and the events recorded. Think about the people the passage mentions – their responses, their personalities. Look at the context of the passage. As you do this, ask God to speak to *you* through it.

3. Now work through each question in the study. Think what the question is getting at. Chew over the passage in the light of it. Jot down as full an answer as you can. This will help you clarify it in your own mind, so that you can contribute to the group yourself.

4. Consult the explanatory notes in the study itself, the Leader's Notes relating to the study (pp. 101ff.) and the Word List at the end of this book. You could also use some of the books listed on p. 123 to add to your own understanding of the passage. Note particularly the 'Goal(s)' for each study, set out in the Leader's Notes.

5. Each study begins with a question headed 'Opening up'. This question is intended to get group members thinking about 'where they are coming from' as they encounter the specified passage in Luke. It also aims to get the group to open up to one another so as to encourage a deeper level of relationship and fellowship. Group members will take their cue from you, so do be ready to open up yourself. The more you share, the more they will.

When you meet

1. Ensure that each group member has a copy of the study guide and a Bible. The studies are based on the New International Version, so it's best if you all have a copy of that version. But have other modern versions on hand too – they might help you to understand a difficult passage, or shed more light on a passage you thought you had understood.

2. Make sure everyone is comfortable and knows one another, and that someone will have coffee and biscuits (or whatever) ready at the end.

3. Begin and end on time. Don't let the meeting go on too long (especially if you're using someone else's house or room);

people may have a bus to catch, or may need to get up early next morning. You may need to select which questions you tackle in each study in order to fit in with your time constraints.

4. Open and close each study with prayer, first that God will help each of you to hear and receive his Word, and then that he will empower you to act upon it. Don't forget to thank God for the privilege of meeting together to study his Word. You could get a group member to open and/or close in prayer; but unless you're *sure* the person doesn't mind having this sprung on him or her, it's best to arrange this in advance, especially for the first few meetings. If someone wants to write down a prayer beforehand, that's fine.

5. At the beginning of your first meeting, explain that the sessions are meant to be discussions, not lectures. Encourage everyone to take part and chip in (but be careful not to embarrass shy members). In order to get the quieter members used to hearing the sound of their own voice in the group, you could ask them (in advance) if they could help you by reading aloud the passage in Luke, or some other set element of the study, such as the questions. You could also ask each group member (quiet *and* talkative) to get the ball rolling with their answers to one or more of the 'Exploring the story' questions, *but*

- ask them in advance, and
- don't do it for the first one or two meetings, till people feel sufficiently relaxed to do this.

6. In order to focus everyone's mind on the topic of the study, read out (or get someone to read out) the introductory section.

7. Give others the chance to answer each question before you do. Welcome all answers, comments and subsidiary questions if at all possible. Avoid making anyone feel silly or rejected because of what they have said. If someone says something that is clearly off course, you could respond, 'Whereabouts in the passage do you see that?' or 'What do the rest of you think?' or 'It might be best if we talked about that after the meeting; I'd rather stick to the main point just now.'

8. Don't be content with just one answer to a question. Several people might have different insights or see different ways of applying the passage to life today. Ask 'Anyone else?' or 'What do others think?' or (for instance) 'What do you think verse 6 adds to what's already been said on that?'

9. Don't be frightened of silences. People need time to think. But if it's an *awkward* silence, it could be that people haven't understood the question, or the verse(s) in Luke to which it relates. Try asking: 'Anyone got any ideas on what this question's getting at?' Or rephrase it: 'I think this question is meant to help us find out . . .'

10. Don't feel you have to stick rigidly to the study guide. If a question has already been answered in the course of answering an earlier one, move on to the next one. If someone raises an important question not covered in the study guide, and you feel it would be valuable *for the group* to discuss it, do so (but see 7, above).

11. Don't worry if people disagree, or if the group doesn't resolve an issue to everyone's satisfaction. The problem might get sorted out in a later session. If animosity threatens, intervene to move on to the next point. Often a touch of humour will relieve tension: 'Order, order! Can we move on, please?' or 'I think you two had better fight this one out after the meeting! Meanwhile, can we go to the next question . . .?'

12. It's helpful if every now and then, and at the end, you summarize what the group has said about the passage. This helps people see where they have reached, fixes the main points in their minds, and sets the next questions (or the next session) in context.

13. Allow plenty of time for the 'Thinking back' questions, which aim to help people see how the passage applies to them and how they can act on what they've learnt. Again, it will encourage others to share openly if you yourself are open about the way God has spoken to you.

14. Remember:

● This is not an exam; there's no pass or fail mark.

- It's not a competition; the aim is not to see who can regurgitate the most detailed information, but to hear God speak.
- No-one expects you as leader to know all the answers to every question anyone might ask. If you don't know, admit it, and go on a voyage of discovery with the person who asked it. Books, an older Christian or a minister might be able to help.
- God *wants* to speak through your study of the passage, so you've got everything going for you!

Leader's notes

Study 1: People at the beginning of the story

Goals for the study

Group members will have a variety of impressions of the Christmas story. This study should challenge such impressions, causing change as they come under the scrutiny of the biblical narrative.

Mary and the shepherds reacted differently to their first encounter with Jesus. Members of the group will be provoked to think about their reactions to new situations.

1 and 11. The opening activity (thinking about Christmas cards) is to begin where people will have opinions and experiences already. The purpose of the final activity is to demonstrate that for some (if not all) there will have been change and progress in their understanding – something we would want to happen at every group meeting! In a group you can share the different images that group members have thought of.

> When you read the passage in a group you could appoint a narrator and other people to read the speech of the different characters (as long as you are using the same version). This involves more people and helps to bring the story alive.

2. Verse 27. For an explanation of the virgin birth have a look at the section on 'Miracles', p. 45.

---

7. It is important to allow plenty of time for reflection and prayer at this point. How well group members know each other will affect how open people will be with each other.

8. Angels, who appear a lot in the birth narrative, were the traditional messengers from God (see also Luke 1:11; Matthew 1:20; 2:13, 19). On verse 11, See the reference in the Word List to *Christ*.

Study 2: Jesus and John the Baptist

Goal for the study

This study contrasts the complementary roles of Jesus and John the Baptist. In the process, group members should explore the questions that they too may be asking about Jesus in the hope of finding a way forward.

2a. See note on *Zechariah* in the Word List. These particular duties in the temple may have been a once-in-a-lifetime opportunity.

2b. See note on *Circumcision*. It was unusual to name the child at the same time as circumcision. But to combine the two events gave a larger audience for the recovery of Zechariah's power of speech.

5. If you are leading a student group, most members will not be parents. Encourage them to pray for parents they know in their families or churches. You could pray for the wider Christian church; for example, parents in war-torn countries or places of particular hardship.

> For variety, ask one person to read the verses in Luke 3 while the rest of the group listen with their eyes closed. Encourage them to picture the scene of Jesus' baptism. This can lead on to answering question 6.

9. Maybe John, in prison, did not see the dramatic impact of Jesus' ministry which he had been expecting. Some have even felt he was unhappy about Jesus' reduced emphasis on judgment, although it was there in 11:13–14, 37–53.

11. In a group, share the questions people have raised. How might you help each other find answers? For instance, how accessible to group members are Bible dictionaries or commentaries? How available are older Christians to advise you? How can you pray for each other in this respect or share your own searches for understanding?

Study 3: Satanic attack and evil spirits

Goals for the study
To learn from Jesus' example about how to face temptation, and to explore what his encounter with demon possession has to teach us today.

1. This opening question is intended to get you thinking and prepare you for the possible surprise of what this passage reveals about the nature of evil.

> When reading Luke 4:1–13 you could ask the tallest member of your group to read the devil's words, and the shortest to read those of Jesus. You or another could read the narrator's words. The tall/short contrast will help to highlight the chosen vulnerability of Jesus. 1 Samuel 16:7 makes it clear that outward appearances are by no means the whole story.

2. Of all the gospel writers, Luke makes a special point of focusing on the activity of the Holy Spirit. Draw out the point that to be full of the Holy Spirit and subject to his leading does not guarantee a quiet life – far from it! One of the reasons we receive the gift of the Spirit in the first place is to enable us to stand firm under the onslaught of evil, not to avoid it altogether.

3. The subtlety of this temptation lies in the condition attached to it – 'If you are the Son of God . . .' (verse 3). As Howard Marshall comments, 'Jesus is being tempted to use his power as Son of God for his own ends instead of being obedient to the Father' (*The Gospel of Luke: A Commentary on the Greek Text*, Paternoster, 1978, p. 170). To have sought further proof of his identity by performing the miracle would have been to demonstrate a lack of trust in the affirmation he had received after his baptism (see 3:22).

4. Jesus' response is to use Scripture. But notice verse 10 – the devil can quote the Bible too! Scripture must be used properly, in context, not twisted to mean what we want it to mean.

5. Encourage the group to reflect on the reality of the onslaught Jesus faced in his long conflict with the devil. Notice especially verse 2. Bishop Westcott, commenting on Hebrews 2:18, makes this telling point: 'Sympathy with the sinner in his trial does not depend on the experience of sin, but on the experience of the strength of temptation to sin, which only the sinless can know in its full intensity. He who fails yields before the last strain' (quoted by Norval Geldenhuys, *The Gospel of Luke*, Marshall, Morgan and Scott, 1951).

6. Each of these temptations seeks to undermine the relationship of trust and obedience which Jesus had with his heavenly Father. As Jesus makes clear in John's gospel, the essence of sin is unbelief (see John 16:9). The extent to which we see unbelief as evil is a good indicator of the extent to which we share God's perspective on what sin really is.

7. Draw out the ways in which the story shows this man to be controlled against his will. There's all the difference in the world between being 'possessed' by an evil spirit and 'filled' with the Holy Spirit; see, for example, 1 Corinthians 14:32–33.

8. Notice here the evil spirit's supernatural recognition of the identity of Jesus as 'the Holy One of God' (verse 34). More important, though, is Jesus' attitude in addressing the evil spirit as a separate and personal entity. The people's amazement in verse 36 shows clearly that something visible and significant must have happened to the man as a result of this encounter.

9. You could use this question in particular as a basis for quiet reflection and prayer.

10. Jesus' desire to conceal his true identity as the 'Christ' or 'Messiah' is related to the fact that contemporary expectations of what that meant were rather different from what the prophets in the Old Testament had revealed. The cosmic and all-embracing scope of the latter had shrunk to the narrow expectation that the primary role of the Messiah was political: to set his people free from domination by the occupying Roman power. For Jesus, the 'good news of the kingdom of God' (verse 43) meant much more than this.

Study 4: The disciples

Goal for the study
To learn how to follow Jesus more closely from what Luke writes about his pattern of life and ministry.

1. This opening question is designed to get the group thinking about the possible gap between what they think of as discipleship and what the Bible actually indicates about it. We tend to think that to be a Christian is one thing, but that to be a disciple is rather more demanding. Such a distinction would have been unknown in the early church (see Acts 11:26).

In reading the various passages you could bring a variety of translations, one for each section. The group could follow all the readings in the NIV. You could then have the opportunity to make the point that the gospel was originally written in Greek, and that translations from one language to another naturally vary.

2. Draw out the sense of conflict expressed in verse 5. On the one hand, Simon has already seen evidence of the miraculous power of Jesus, even in his own family (see 4:38–39). On the other hand, here is Jesus 'interfering' in an area where Simon is an expert!

3. Here is one of the primary marks by which disciples may be identified: obedience to the one they are seeking to follow. The point is that although God sometimes tells us why he wants us to do something, he doesn't always do so. Some group members may like to share examples from their own experience. In talking through how God's voice may be identified, bear in mind the privilege each Christian has to hear God personally (see John 10:27) and the importance of Bible study, prayer and the input of other Christians to confirm what we sense God is saying to us.

4. This is a very important lesson for disciples to learn. If the Son of God needed to spend so much time in prayer, how much more do we! When group members have shared their experiences in this area, you might like to pause and pray for one another.

5. Although it's sometimes possible to make a direct link between disease and past sin, we often can't make this connection. Indeed, such a straightforward link between sin and misfortune is explicitly denied by Jesus in Luke 13:1–5. In Luke 5, the point is not so much that the man's sin caused his disease but that his sin was at least as significant a problem as his paralysis.

6. Use the opportunity given by this question to welcome the testimonies of how group members discovered (or are discovering) who Jesus is.

7. Tax-collectors are lumped together with more obvious 'sinners' because they collaborated with the occupying Roman power (and so were regarded as ceremonially unclean) and because they often took more by way of commission than was just. See the story of Zacchaeus in Luke 19:2–10.

8. The key aspects to draw out is what it means for us to 'leave everything' and follow Jesus. How radical should we be now? How radical should we seek to remain? Choose a practical example to discuss, like whether it's right for a disciple of Jesus to own a house.

9. Draw out the different ways in which Jesus overturns the expectations of what, according to the Pharisees, a good religious teacher should be like. Worse still, he is able to prove the truth of what he says by what he does. Luke 13:17 provides a pithy summary of the situation.

10. The parable refers back to the objection in verse 33. Jesus' focus is on the inner reality of the kingdom of God, a reality which is all too easily obscured by concentrating on the minutiae of external religious observance. Encourage group members to think of ways in which their 'religion' interferes with their 'faith'.

12. The word 'apostle' means 'sent one'. Mark gives us a little more detail about what being an apostle meant in Mark 3:14–15. As you answer this question, make the most of the opportunity to pray for those in the group who are facing major decisions at the moment.

Study 5: Faith and the non-Jew

Goal for the study
To learn how to have the sort of faith that would amaze Jesus.

1. This is a hard but worthwhile question to face up to. If group members are reticent about their own prejudices, draw out those that they are aware of in others. In overcoming prejudice, there is no substitute for personal relationship.

> When reading Luke 7:10 you could assign various parts to group members – the narrator (Luke), the elders of the Jews, the friends of the centurion, and Jesus. Make sure all are using the same translation.

2. There are a number of aspects to draw out: his standing as a centurion, the high value he places on his servant's life, his concern for the welfare of those in the country he and his men are occupying, his humility in the way he approached Jesus, his ability to relate his day-to-day experience to spiritual reality.

4. Notice the contrast between what the centurion thought about himself (verse 7) and what the elders of the Jews thought about him (verse 4). The genuineness of his humility is demonstrated by his attitude in sending a second delegation with the message that Jesus should not trouble himself.

5. Just like us, the centurion has never seen Jesus but has to rely on what he has heard about him. Give group members the opportunity to talk about how they and, perhaps, their friends find it difficult to believe without seeing evidence for themselves.

6. Notice how the centurion addresses Jesus in verse 6 and his dominant concern with authority.

7. For Jesus, this man must have been a refreshing change from all those who came to him simply in order to witness something spectacular take place. Here is someone whose faith is uncontaminated by the need to see.

Jesus says that not even in Israel – that is, among God's chosen people, who had the Old Testament Bible and a strong tradition of worship – had he encountered such unquestioning faith as was demonstrated by this Gentile. Even we Christians sometimes hesitate to believe that if God says it, it'll happen!

9. For one thing, we can learn to *expect* faith to be more a matter of trusting the one we cannot see than relying on what we can see. Notice too the clear grasp the centurion has of the principle of authority. Just as he does not have to be visible for his soldiers to obey him, so Jesus does not have to be visible for a sickness to obey him.

Study 6: Jesus and social misfits

Goals for the study
To see how Jesus' love extended to the most unexpected people, and to build faith that no-one is beyond his reach today.

1, 4 and 8. 'He/she's the *last* person who'll ever become a Christian!' We all know people of whom we think that. This study aims to encourage group members to realize that no-one is beyond the pale for God. Get them to think of specific people, and to be honest about their doubts. Encourage them to pray for those people.

2. Remember that there was no social-security system and few 'career opportunities' for women; widows were therefore often among the most vulnerable members of society, dependent on relatives to provide for their needs. Here we see Jesus 'following in his Father's footsteps' in demonstrating care for this widow; you could get three group members to read aloud Psalm 68:5; Psalm 146:9 and Proverbs 15:25. Later, the early church saw its obligation to make provision for widows; see Acts 6:1–4; 1 Timothy 5:9–10; James 1:27. You could think about who are today's vulnerable members of society and how Christians and churches can demonstrate Jesus' compassion to them.

3. Ritual uncleanness meant that a man could not participate in service in the temple sanctuary and could not enjoy fellowship with other Jews until he had undergone the appropriate form of cleansing. The most defiling thing anyone could do was to touch a dead human body or something that had been in contact with a body. For the implications of Jesus' action here, get someone to read out Numbers 19:11–13, 17–22.

4. Maybe group members would like to tell the others about 'impossible' situations in their experience where God's deliverance has been demonstrated.

When reading the passage concerning the sinful women you could spray enough perfume for the fragrance to be quite strongly sensed. (Check first that this won't cause problems, *e.g.* to people with asthma.)

---

5 and 7. To get an idea of the contrast between the woman and Simon, take today's gender discrimination and magnify it a good many times! Add to it the fact that the Pharisees' chief concern was meticulous observance of the Old Testament law, and that that law abominated prostitution and prescribed the death penalty for it (see Leviticus 21:9; Deuteronomy 22:20–21). The Old Testament prophets often used the image of prostitution to refer to the great evil of apostasy – unfaithfulness to the Lord and the giving of oneself to other gods (*e.g.* Isaiah 57:3–8; Jeremiah 3:1–5; Hosea 2:2–13). You can imagine the depths of horror Simon must have felt on this occasion!

6. The woman's perfumed ointment was very costly, containing spikenard, a herb imported from North India. It was preserved in alabaster flasks, and, like a good wine today, it improved with age and increased in value. The actions which Simon failed to perform (verses 44–46) were the equivalent of our welcoming hug or handshake and our 'Come in! Sit down! I'll put the kettle on', in a hot, dusty land where people wore open sandals and walked, or travelled by donkey, on dirt roads. The kiss would be like the ones we see on TV news reports when Middle Eastern leaders meet. The oil would have been olive oil, much cheaper than the perfumed ointment used by the repentant woman.

8. Jesus isn't saying that some people have less need of forgiveness than others, but that some people more fully appreciate the depth of their sin and hence the depth of God's forgiveness. 'Respectable' people, whose sinfulness may centre more on inward things such as pride and lack of compassion, equally need forgiveness. Jesus' tone is one of gentle irony.

11. In all honesty, Christians have to admit that some later manifestations of Christianity *have* devalued women. But this contrasts with the radically non-chauvinist attitude of Jesus.

Study 7: Among the crowds

Goal for the study
To look at the ways Jesus ministered to others and coped with the

demands made on him, so that we can apply what we learn to our own Christian service.

1. Some group members might feel that because they are quieter and don't relish a public arena, they're not much use to God. Encourage them to see that the more intimate forms of Christian service, to which they may be ideally suited, are equally valuable. Maybe some of the extraverts in the group, too, need to learn to appreciate the strengths of their quieter brothers and sisters.

In order to let Jesus' words make their maximum impact on the group, you could get one person to read the passage slowly and expressively, with plenty of time between each beatitude to allow the members to meditate on and pray about each one.

---

2. Get the group to look at a scale map of the Holy Land in the time of Jesus (there's probably one in the back of their Bibles) to see how large an area is covered by the description in verse 17. This 'sermon on the plain' was probably delivered somewhere near Capernaum in the region of Galilee.

2, 3 and 9. Encourage group members to share strategies they have found helpful, for the benefit of others in the group.

4. This is almost certainly another account of Matthew's 'sermon on the mount' (Matthew 5 – 7), rather than a separate teaching occasion (see the entry in the *New Bible Dictionary*, IVP, 2nd edition, 1982).

5. Encourage group members to discuss how widely they think these ideals should be, or can be, applied. Is Jesus talking about relationships 'in the kingdom', or is he asking us to behave like this in all our relationships? Where do law and order fit in? See the discussion in the *New Bible Dictionary* article already mentioned.

Verse 31: The famous 'Golden Rule' echoes the exhortation in Leviticus 19:18, 'Love your neighbour as yourself', which Jesus (Mark 12:29–31) and Paul (Romans 13:9; Galatians 5:14) regarded as encapsulating the whole law relating to our dealings with others. Similar sayings are found in other religions, but usually in a negative form (*e.g.* 'Let no man do to another any act he wishes not done to himself', in the Hindu *Mahabharata*).

Verse 32: The term "sinners" referred, not to specially bad people, but to ordinary people who were not particularly rigorous in their observance of the religious laws, or whose job or trade entailed ritual uncleanness – and, of course, to non-Jews.

Verses 35–36: Jesus is not alone in the Bible in calling us to imitate God; see, *e.g.*, Leviticus 19:1, Ephesians 5:1. Our destiny as Christians is to be like Christ, who is the exact representation of God (1 John 3:2; Hebrews 1:3). He is not suggesting in verse 35 that we *earn* our status as God's children by loving our enemies, but that by doing so we demonstrate that we *are* God's children. '"Son of" is an idiom for "having the characteristics of" or "doing the work of"' (article 'Sons [children] of God' in the *New Bible Dictionary*).

6. Verse 42 is often cited as an example of Jesus' humour. Note how, in verses 37–49, Jesus communicates his teaching in ways which would easily resonate with his hearers and relate to their everyday experience.

9. For examples of Jesus' withdrawing to pray, alone or with a small group of disciples, see Luke 5:16; 6:12; 9:28; 11:1; and 21:37 with 22:39–40.

10. This question can be answered in two complementary ways. Think about (a) the benefits to the disciples of being involved in a 'hands-on' way in what Jesus was doing, and (b) the benefits to Jesus too. (Are we ever tempted to think 'we can handle it' on our own? What lies behind this? What example does Jesus set us here?)

Study 8: Jesus and religious people

Goals for the study
To explore what qualifies us to know God and do his will; and to examine how Jesus deals with religious people.

1. The aim of this question is to get the group thinking about the fact that we are accepted by God because of what Christ has done for us on the cross. Our acceptance by God is not as a result of birth, religious background, status or obedience to rules and regulations, whether of scriptural or human origin, but through the grace of God. The free gift of forgiveness is received by faith. We cannot earn it.

2. Perhaps one group member could be asked to start off with a summary or the 'gist' of the passage, with other members being encouraged to chip in once a good start has been made.

3. The fact that the Pharisees (see the entry in the Word List) and experts in the law were present and are described as carefully watching Jesus (verse 1) may indicate that this was a trap. They wanted to see if they could catch Jesus out on his obedience to the religious laws. It is possible that the ill man whom Jesus healed was brought in deliberately so that they could watch what Jesus would do with him.

4. The rule that it was not lawful to heal on the Sabbath was not a biblical one. It arose instead from their own *rabbinical* (see *Rabbi* in the Word List) religious rules which in the Jews' view prevented them from doing good on the Sabbath. If they agreed with him, they would in effect be saying that their own religious rule was wrong. If they contradicted his argument that it was 'lawful' to heal on the Sabbath, they would be contradicting Scripture, which does not prohibit healing on the Sabbath. Jesus' use of the word 'lawful' (verse 3) refers to the law of Moses (see the Word List under *Law*) Accordingly Jesus would have been able to prove them wrong either way. Their readiness to stick to their rabbinical rules rendered them, in practice, indifferent to human suffering.

5. Encourage the group to think deeply about this question if their first reaction is that they are unable to think of any.

6. Where you sat at such a social gathering said an enormous amount about your social status and importance. It often showed who had power – or who was seeking it. Accordingly, the guests at the meal may have scrambled for the best places, being concerned always to improve or maintain their status in the eyes of those around them. Jesus instead advocates genuine humility. As a wedding feast was a symbol of the kingdom of God, Jesus may have been pointing out that those who by reason of their religious status expect to be put in prime positions may in fact be humiliated, and the genuinely humble will be exalted by God (see *New Bible Commentary*, p. 1004).

7. Encourage the group to apply the question to their personal circumstances and relationships.

8. The excuses given mask the fact that those invited do not want to go.

9. Jesus had in effect said to the Pharisees and teachers of the law that their obedience to rules, merit, status and jockeying for position in the religious hierarchy would not get them to the wedding feast. Instead those whom they considered 'sinners' (see for example Luke 15:1–2) would be invited in their place.

In this session, the group may bring up attitudes of pride or legalism which they need to repent of and confess. Often we can accept what Jesus has done for us as the basis of our salvation, but still feel that we have to win favour with God by what we do. What we do for God matters, but obedience should be the result of being made right with God, not the way we gain acceptance from him.

Study 9: Jesus and his captors

Goals for the study
To understand the conflict going on behind the human events leading up to the cross, and to examine the way Jesus dealt with his captors and those who betrayed him.

1. While the disciples frequently failed to understand Jesus' ministry and ultimate objective, their understanding does grow slowly as Luke's story progresses. Note that Luke 22:45 does point to some realization on the part of the disciples that Jesus' death may be imminent.

> You could ask a group member beforehand to prepare to read the passage for this session. By now you will know which members read aloud better than others. Try to chose a particularly good reader.

2. The extreme agony of Jesus' prayer time on the Mount of Olives arose from his struggle with the temptation to back off from carrying out his Father's will. Because he went to face arrest, trial and crucifixion completely secure in God's will and approval, he could face the betrayal, torture and humiliation that the next hours would bring. (He also knew that in going to the cross he would go alone; only he could be the sacrifice for sin.) So his acceptance of what his friends and captors did to him was not from weakness, but from strength. In that strength he was able to be uniquely vulnerable, and to withstand the enormous temptation which he must have felt to fight back. Note the hypocrisy of Judas using a kiss, the sign of affection, as a means of identifying Jesus to those who came to arrest him, and also the compassion of Christ in healing the servant's ear.

3. Note particularly their failure to pray (verse 46) and their readiness to use physical force (verses 49–50).

4. Jesus' prayer in verse 42 often causes some confusion. It was an inevitable product of Jesus' humanity that he temporarily sacrificed the ability to know everything ('omniscience') to live within the limitations of a human body (although, miraculously, without compromising his divine perfection). Accordingly, prayer, for him as for us, involved seeking the will of the Father. If he knew everything he would not have needed to pray. We presume he struggled with whether or not he had to endure the suffering of the cross, and that as he prayed he saw more clearly that it was God's will. Some commentators observe that this verse shows us that Jesus experienced the lack of an answer to his prayer (more correctly, to the first clause of it). Sometimes our prayers are not answered because they are wrong. Jesus could not be wrong because of sin – he was perfect. Instead, his prayer was part of the process of subjecting himself to the will of God – hence the second clause of the prayer.

5. Encourage group members to put themselves in the position of the slave and those around him who saw what was going on (including the disciples present). One point that is often made from this story is that there are times when Christians are too aggressive in evangelism and turn their hearers away from the gospel because of their unpleasantness. Presumably having your ear cut off by someone who was a follower of Christ would not incline you towards Christianity. By healing him, Jesus enabled the slave to remain able to listen and, potentially, to be receptive to the good news of Jesus at some future point.

6. Jesus clearly saw the eternal implications of what was going on, and that he had to go to the cross. He also knew the means by which he would be sent. He understood that while his captors acted with full moral responsibility for their actions, they were unwittingly fulfilling God's purpose of sending Christ to the cross. Luke records in Acts 4:27–28 that the early church saw in retrospect that the Jewish and Roman authorities, although they acted in accordance with their sinful desires, brought about the crucifixion of Christ ultimately because it was God's purpose.

7. Encourage the group to be honest. Remember that we can easily deny Christ by our actions as much as by our words.

9. Ultimately Jesus' perfection is the reason anyone would have sent him to the cross. If we love darkness, we shall flee the light – or try to extinguish it.

According to Leon Morris (*Luke*, p. 319), the Jewish leaders found Jesus an embarrassing inconvenience because

- the Pharisees saw him as a blasphemer;
- he had seriously rebuked the religious establishment for its hypocrisy;
- the high priest's revenue would have suffered when Jesus cleared the temple;
- his existence was politically inconvenient for the Jews *vis-à-vis* the Romans – he might cause the Romans to take away what little power the Romans had devolved to the Jews;
- Jesus claimed to be the Son of God, which they viewed as blasphemy.

10. Leon Morris comments on verses 67–69 that 'the council invites Jesus to incriminate himself by telling them that he was the Messiah' (*Luke*, p. 317), and that Jesus' understanding of the nature of the Messiah was so different from theirs that even if he explained it they would not understand it. In Luke 20 Jesus had asked them about the Messiah, but they had failed to answer. He assumes that they will not reply again (verse 68). Jesus' admission (verse 70) to being the Son of God (which of course he was, although the Jews could not see that) was for them sufficient to incriminate him on a charge of blasphemy.

Spend some time praying for the group's deepening understanding of Jesus' death and resurrection, and how their understanding of it affects their faith and evangelism. The death and resurrection are, of course, absolutely central to our belief and action. You may particularly wish to pray for boldness for those in the group who are timid in sharing their faith.

Study 10: The risen Jesus and his friends

Goal for the study
To explore the evidence for the resurrection.

1. Two common factors are that people rediscover – or discover for the first time – the trustworthiness of the Bible. They find that its truth clarifies their confusion and enables them to be confident in the God it reveals and in what he promises. Additionally, or alternatively, they see again the meaning of Christ's sacrifice and love for them – in a sense they meet Christ afresh. Remember that some doubt is healthy!

For the Bible reading in this section try to obtain beforehand the NIV translation of Luke on audiotape, published by Hodder Headline, and narrated by Tenniel Evans. Play the relevant section, or even the whole chapter. Your church or CU may be willing to purchase the two audiotapes.

---

2. Some people who notionally accept the idea of the resurrection think that it was merely a spiritual resurrection, and that the post-crucifixion Jesus did not have a physical body. This is contrary to passages such as this, where clear evidence is put forward for Christ's body being physical (even if it had some unusual characteristics, such as the ability to 'disappear' in verse 31). Orthodox Christian belief has always been unequivocal about Jesus' physical resurrection. Evidence in this passage for the physical resurrection of Christ includes the following:

- verse 15: Jesus physically appears to the two disciples
- verse 23: the disappeared body
- verse 36: he appears to the main group of disciples
- verses 39, 40: he invites the disciples to touch his body
- verse 43: Jesus eats fish

3. Note their partial belief in the prophets, which did not take into account the prophecies that the Messiah would suffer. The inevitable emotional trauma and grief of Christ's death would also have contributed to their demoralized state.

4. We do not have a definite answer to this question from the text. However, it is possible that Jesus wanted them to develop in their understanding of the Scriptures before their intellectual belief was confirmed in the experience of meeting him.

5. The critical distinction is that the prophet offers no sacrifice for sin; that was the role of the priest in Old Testament worship. Jesus' supreme sacrifice of himself is the only mechanism for salvation. The prophet came to declare God's truth in the Old Testament. (See the section on 'Salvation', p. 60.)

6. Note how he points out their limited knowledge and application of the Old Testament Scriptures to which they had access. Note particularly verses 25 and 27, where he insists that they should believe *all* the Prophets and Scriptures. They had failed to look at the whole Old Testament picture. 'The two had a wrong idea of what the Old Testament thought and thus they had a wrong idea about the cross' (Leon Morris, *Luke*, p. 339).

7. Sensitive to their inevitable grief, Christ's questioning draws out their concerns (verses 17, 19); he clarifies their understanding (verses 25ff., 44); greets them as a bringer of peace in the midst of their fear (verse 36); and offers them physical proof of his reality to confirm that he is not a ghost (verses 39, 40, 42).

8. 'Will the real Jesus of Nazareth please stand up? Where are we to find him? There is only one answer, and that is in the God-authorized documents that speak of him ... it must be "according to the Scriptures", because there is no other Jesus to confess. Any other Jesus is an imposter' (Roy Clements in John White *et al.*, *Hear the Word*, IVP, 1990, pp. 102–103). Jesus himself had reminded them of the scriptural description of the Messiah and what he would achieve, so that they could see that he was the one promised in the Scriptures.

Uniquely, too (and unlike us) they would have physically recognized him and his wounds; they subjectively knew that they were in his presence (verse 32). They knew his voice (John 10:27).

9. The group may find it helpful to split into twos or threes to write down the ways they would explain the cross and resurrection. The aim of this question is to help the group members feel more confident in explaining this central aspect of the Christian message to their friends. After discussion, spend some time praying together about the cross and thanking Christ for what he achieved there for us.

10. If we underemphasize the role and place of Scripture we lose the unchanging yardstick by which we are to measure all thought and experience, so as to be able to discern truth and error. Our faith runs the risk of losing sight of the objective truth of Christianity; Christianity is then reduced to merely an alternative spiritual experience which is simply 'better' than other people's. If we undervalue our experience of God, we run the risk of making our Christianity mechanical and the truth clinical and loveless. In truth we cannot separate the Word of God from the breath that carries it. (For further reading on this issue see chapters 5 and 6 of *Hear the Word*.)

Background reading

John Blanchard, *Luke Comes Alive!* (Evangelical Press, 1986).

D. A. Carson *et al.* (eds.), *New Bible Commentary*, 21st Century Edition (IVP, 1994).

Leon Morris, *Luke*, Tyndale Commentary (IVP, 1974).

Michael Wilcock, *The Message of Luke*, The Bible Speaks Today series (IVP, 1979).

Word list

People and places appearing in Luke

Angel A divine messenger appearing in human form but obviously supernatural. The one who spoke to Mary and to Zechariah was named as Gabriel.

Annas Appointed high priest AD 6 and deposed AD 15, yet still referred to as high priest afterwards.

Barabbas Arrested for political terrorism, and released by Pilate as a substitute for Jesus.

Bethany A village about 3 km from Jerusalem, the home of Mary and Martha.

Bethlehem A town 8 km south-west of Jerusalem, in the Judean hills, and birthplace of Jesus.

Caiaphas High priest AD 18–36, working in close cooperation with his father-in-law, Annas.

Capernaum An important fishing town on the north-west shore of the Lake of Galilee, and Jesus' base while teaching in the region. Levi lived here, as well as Peter's family.

Christ A term for the Messiah. See *Jesus.*

Elizabeth Wife of Zechariah the priest, and mother of John the Baptist. She was a relation of Mary, the mother of Jesus.

Emmaus A village about 13 km from Jerusalem.

Galilee A region in northern Israel which included the large lake of Galilee and Jesus' home town, Nazareth. Much of Jesus' teaching and healing took place here.

Herod Title of the king or ruler of the Jews, but having little actual power during the Roman occupation.

James, the disciple A son of Zebedee, and brother of John, who abandoned his fishing trade to join Jesus' band of disciples.

Jericho One of the world's ancient towns, located 250 m below sea level about 8 km north of the Dead Sea.

Jerusalem Capital city and spiritual centre of the ancient Jewish kingdom. Jerusalem stands 770 m high in the Judean hills. In Jesus' day the temple was located there; it was destroyed by the Romans in AD 70.

Jesus The name means 'saviour' or 'rescuer'. He is the subject of Luke's gospel, born 4–6 BC and died probably AD 33. Luke records Jesus' divine origin, fully human nature, and triumph over death as Son of God.

John the Baptist A prophet sent to herald the coming of his cousin, Jesus, as God's Messiah. John baptized Jesus and died at the hands of Herod.

John, the disciple A son of Zebedee, and brother of James. Both brothers were in their father's fishing business in Galilee when Jesus called them. Author of several New Testament books, including a gospel.

Joseph Legal father of Jesus, a carpenter by trade. Luke records Jesus' miraculous conception by Mary, whom Joseph married.

Joseph of Arimathea A secret disciple of Jesus, and member of the council of elders. He provided his tomb for Jesus.

Judas Iscariot The disciple who betrayed Jesus, and came probably from Kerioth, hence, Iscariot. He was responsible for the finances of the band of disciples.

Judea A region of Palestine, the others being Samaria and Galilee. It was considered the most orthodox region.

Korazin A village on the Lake of Galilee.

Lake of Galilee A large lake (21 km long and 11 km broad) in the region of Galilee, kept fresh by the River Jordan running through it. Surrounded by hills, it is liable to atmospheric down-drafts and sudden storms. The lake plays an important part in Luke's story.

Lake of Gennesaret Another name of the Lake of Galilee.

Lazarus The beggar in Jesus' story of the rich man and the beggar.

Levi Also called Matthew, a tax-collector who abandoned his trade to follow Jesus as one of his band of disciples. He is author of a New Testament gospel.

Martha The hospitable sister of Mary of Bethany, and close friend of Jesus.

Mary The sister of Martha of Bethany, and close friend of Jesus.

Mary, the mother of Jesus When Mary conceived Jesus by divine action, she was a virgin engaged to Joseph, who married her when the origin of the pregnancy was revealed to him.

Mount of Olives A hill, 830 m in height, overlooking Jerusalem and its temple area from the east. It was reached by crossing the Kidron Valley.

Nain A village near Nazareth in Galilee where Jesus brought back the life of a widow's son.

Nazareth A town of Galilee where Jesus grew up and plied his trade as a carpenter until he began his ministry of teaching, healing and salvation.

Peter He was a fisherman with his brother Andrew, before joining Jesus' band of disciples. Peter was a natural leader and became the author of two New Testament letters. He is probably the main source of Mark's gospel.

Pilate Appointed as Roman prefect of Judea in AD 26, he was in control of the province, but had a stormy relationship with the Jewish authorities.

Samaria The capital of the northern kingdom of Israel before the exile. The inhabitants of the area (Samaritans) had much in common racially and in religion with the Jews, but there was animosity between the two at the time of Jesus.

Tyre An important coastal port to the north of Palestine.

Zacchaeus A little man of Jericho who climbed a tree in order to see Jesus. He abandoned his job as a tax-collector to become a disciple of Jesus.

Zechariah Husband of Elizabeth and father of John the Baptist. He was a priest who served in the temple. Not to be confused with the prophet (and his Old Testament book) of the same name.

Background to Luke

Abel The Bible's first murder victim, second son of Adam and Eve, the parents of humankind.

Abraham The founder of the Jewish people.

Abyss A region of hell, believed at the time to be in the underworld, where demons are imprisoned, awaiting judgment day.

Alabaster A soft stone material out of which pots, jars and vases were made.

Beelzebub A name for Satan or the devil.

Caesar Roman Emperor Caesar Augustus, great-nephew of Julius Caesar, ruled from 30 BC to AD 14. He was succeeded by his step-son and son-in-law, Tiberius Caesar, emperor throughout Jesus' adult life.

Centurion A Roman army officer responsible for about 100 men.

Circumcision Jewish males were circumcised, as a sign of God's covenant with Israel. Traditionally this was carried out eight days after birth.

Consolation of Israel A reference to the long-promised Messiah or Christ, Saviour of the Jewish people.

Council of the elders The Sanhedrin, the highest Jewish tribunal in Jerusalem. It traditionally originated with the seventy elders who assisted Moses (Numbers 11:16–25).

Covenant A pledge, usually between nations or individuals. The title 'The Old Testament' refers to God's covenant with Israel, which is fulfilled through Jesus Christ's death in the new covenant (Luke 22:20).

Cross A Roman form of drawn-out execution, designed to cause maximum suffering as a deterrent to criminals. To cause his death, Jesus would have been nailed to a cross through his wrists and feet.

Curtain of the temple A huge curtain which divided the outer temple from the inner sanctum. Only the high priest was allowed to go within, once a year on the Day of Atonement.

David Israel's greatest king (*c.* 1000 BC) and ancestor of Jesus Christ. Under David the nation's territory extended to its largest area.

Demon An evil spirit.

Denarius A Roman silver coin which represented a day's wage for the ordinary working man. In Jesus' day Greek, Roman and Jewish coins were in circulation.

Devil The chief spiritual being in opposition to God's intentions for the created world and humankind.

Disciple A pupil or follower. Luke's name for the followers of John the Baptist and of Jesus.

Elijah One of the greatest Old Testament prophets (ninth century BC). John the Baptist is seen in Luke's gospel as the new Elijah.

Elisha Elijah's direct successor, who healed the non-Jewish Naaman of a severe skin disease.

Experts in the law See *Scribes*.

Heaven Often identified at the time with the starry heavens above created by God, but beyond normal human sight, the place where God dwells along with his angels, and all his people after this life. It is the place which perfectly expresses God's will.

Hell (Hades) The after-world of unbelievers separated from God, in contrast to heaven, expressed in images of dreadful torment.

Holy Spirit The third person of the Godhead who is at work in the world.

Isaac Son of Abraham, and one of the patriarchs of the Jewish people.

Isaiah Eighth-century-BC prophet

whose prophecies are recorded in the Old Testament, and much quoted by Luke.

Jacob Grandson of Abraham and son of Isaac, one of the patriarchs of the Jewish people.

Jonah The Old Testament prophet ordered by God to preach to non-Jews in Ninevah. Their subsequent repentance is noted by Jesus (11:29–32).

Kingdom of God The kingdom or rule of God is a central theme of Jesus' teaching. In his life and work God's reign begins to take shape, though its full manifestation lies in the future.

Law usually refers to the first five books of the Old Testament, including Leviticus, and sometimes to the Ten Commandments, given by God to Moses.

Levites Jewish men descended from the tribe of Levi, whose task was to help with the temple worship.

Lot Nephew of the patriarch Abraham who escaped the city of Sodom just before its destruction.

Luke Evidently a doctor by profession and a non-Jew who is author of this gospel and its sequel, the Acts of the Apostles. Both books are addressed to Theophilus.

Mina A valuable coin, worth about three months' wages.

Moses Jewish leader (c. 1250 BC) who led the Israelites out of slavery in Egypt and to whom God gave the Ten Commandments. See *Law*.

Naaman A Syrian general of the ninth century BC who was healed of a disfiguring skin disease by the Jewish prophet Elisha.

Noah Central figure in the Old Testament narrative of the great flood which destroyed most of humankind.

Parable A story employing an extended metaphor from ordinary life, a genre perfected by Jesus, with allegorical elements.

Passover A major Jewish festival celebrating the release of Israelite slaves from Egypt under the leadership of Moses. A key element was the sacrificial death of lambs to turn away the plague of death that afflicted Egypt. The fact that Christ's death coincided with the festival was of great significance.

Pharisees A rigid Jewish religious group of laymen who aimed to apply biblical laws, especially priestly ones, more fundamentally to all areas of life.

Priests Probably as many as 7,000 priests were actively involved in temple worship in Jerusalem in the period of this gospel.

Prophet Someone called by God to proclaim his message to Israel. The writings and teachings of the prophets made up one of the three divisions of the Jewish Scriptures (the Old Testament).

Purification According to Jewish law, childbirth made a woman 'unclean' and in need of ritual purification.

Queen of the South Another name for the Queen of Sheba who visited the ancient king, Solomon, son of David.

Rabbis Men in the Jewish religion with a superior knowledge of biblical and religious law, who had a prominent teaching role, especially in synagogues, Jewish places of worship.

Repentance A complete turnabout from sin and self-rule towards God by an individual, or group of people, illustrated in Jesus' parable of the wasteful son.

Resurrection The raising of the human body from death, particularly seen in Jesus' resurrection, and promised to all believers on Christ's return.

Sabbath The seventh and holy day of the Jewish week, beginning at sunset on the Friday. It was a strict day of rest.

Sadducees An aristocratic and predominantly lay religious group who accepted only the five books of Moses, and were sceptical of supernatural elements of belief such as the resurrection of the body.

Salvation In Luke this refers to rescue from the power and effects of sin by Jesus' death on the cross. This rescue encompasses all aspects of life and therefore leads to human wholeness.

Samaritans A mixed-race people living in Samaria between Judea and Galilee, and despised by Jews.

Sanhedrin Alternatively known as the Council, this was the highest tribunal or court of the Jews. It had civil and (at the time of Christ) limited criminal jurisdiction under Jewish law. See the entry in the *New Bible Dictionary*.

Satan See *Devil*.

Scribes A class of professional students and teachers of the law, particularly of the interpretation and application of Old Testament law. They were the experts in religious tradition and were very opposed to Christ.

Sidon A coastal city of ancient Phoenicia, north of Palestine, razed to the ground around 350 BC.

Sinners Those considered at the time to be beyond the pale of God's concern, and therefore of salvation. These included non-Jews and breakers of the religious laws.

Sodom An archetypal place of evil in the Old Testament, the ancient city is now probably covered by the Dead Sea. It was destroyed as a result of divine judgment.

Son of God An existing title which came to be used of Jesus both as Messiah and as one with his Father, *i.e.* fully divine as well as fully human.

Son of Man Jesus took this title for himself from the Old Testament book of Daniel, where it is used of the coming Messiah.

Synagogue A local Jewish meeting-place of worship and teaching of the law. It was also used for a court, for funeral services, and for political gatherings.

Tax-collectors The Roman occupiers employed Jewish tax-collectors who were considered to be traitors by the people.

Temple The centre of Jewish worship located in Jerusalem and destroyed by the Romans in AD 70. Its importance is reflected in its dominance in Luke's gospel.

Theophilus A name meaning 'friend of God'. It is probable that Luke was addressing an actual Greek person of high-rank, but it could also be a general term for his Christian reader.